# Lingua Franca

## A play

## Peter Nichols

Samuel French — London
www.samuelfrench-london.co.uk

# LINGUA FRANCA

First presented by Cherub Company London in association with Neil McPherson on 13th July 2010 at the Finborough Theatre, London, with the following cast:

| | |
|---|---|
| **Steven Flowers** | Chris New |
| **Gennaro Manetti** | Enzo Cilenti |
| **Peggy Carmichael** | Charlotte Randle |
| **Irena Brentano** | Rula Lenska |
| **Madge Fox** | Abigail McKern |
| **Jestin Overton** | Ian Gelder |
| **Heidi Schumann** | Natalie Walter |

Directed by Michael Gieleta
Designed by James Macnamara

## COPYRIGHT INFORMATION

(See also page ii)

# CHARACTERS

**Steven Flowers**, 25
**Gennaro Manetti**, 30
**Peggy Carmichael**, 30
**Irena Brentano**, 50
**Madge Fox**, 45
**Jestin Overton**, 65
**Heidi Schumann**, 22

Voices of various Italian students

The action of the play takes place in the staff rest room and classrooms of a language school in Florence.
Time: mid-1950s

## ACTING EDITION NOTE

A forward slash (/) indicates that the next character to speak should begin speaking.

# ACT I

## SCENE 1

*A classroom in a language school in Florence. Mid-1950s*

*The stage is in darkness, concealing the upstage scene: a staff rest room. In one side wall there is a door to a washroom (off) with a frosted-glass panel; in the upstage wall is a window with a view of Giotto's bell-tower and the façade of Brunelleschi's cathedral beyond the upper floors of a street in Florence. In the right wall is the main door with a switch next to it, a doorknob and key in a keyhole*

*The rest room is furnished in an institutional way with a practical overhead fan, tables, upright chairs, one couch and a bookcase with books, including a "Dictionary of Quotations" in it. On the walls a timetable, drab formal group photos of earlier teaching staffs; brave attempts at cheer in travel posters of Italian towns. On the tables are text and exercise books and a copy of "A Room With A View". On one table is a selection of knives, forks and spoons used in the lessons and one bread knife*

*Steve Flowers, 25, stands beside this table, in a pool of light. He holds up a table knife, facing a class we only hear*

**Steve** Is this a knife? Yes. This is a knife. (*Pointing at someone in the audience*) Is this a knife?
**Italian Woman 1** Non ho capito.
**Steve** Is this a knife? Yes, this is a knife. Attenzione. Is this a knife?
**Italian woman 1** Yes. This is a knife.
**Steve** (*pointing at someone else*) Is this a knife?
**Italian man** Yes. This un'naif.

*Steve smiles and nods, then points at another*

**Steve** What is this?
**Italian Woman 2** Is this a knife?
**Steve** (*shaking his head, repeating*) No. This *is* a knife. Ripété! (*He points again*)

**Italian Woman 2** This is a knife.
**Steve** Bravo! Molto bene!

*He changes the knife for a spoon*

What is this? Is this a knife?

*Confused voices: yes, no, sì, non, knife, che cosa? Etc. Steve stops them*

No, this is not a knife. This is a spoon. Is this a spoon?
**Italian Woman 2** Yes. This is a spoon.

*He nods and changes the spoon for a fork*

**Steve** Benissimo! Is this a spoon? No. This is not a spoon. What is this?
This is a fork. Una forchetta, sì? E questa — una cucchiaio, sì? ... Uno,
sì. Cosa c'é?
**Italian Man** Cucchiaio.
**Steve** But in English? In Inglese?
**Italian Man** Eshpoon?
**Steve** This is a spoon.
**Italian Man** This is un eshpoon.
**Steve** OK. Close. Una coltella, una forchetta, un cucchiaio. Con questa
forchetta io mangio molto pasta. Sì?

*Female laughter bursts out, then is stifled. Steve smiles*

Not right? My pronunciation? La mia pronuncia Italiana non e
abbastanza buona? (*Correcting himself*) Bene?

*He waits. The male speaks fast in Italian and the girls laugh*

What's so funny? Uh? Cosa si buffo? Perché — um — why are you
laughing? (*Losing his cool*) Because I try to speak Italiano? It's not half
as buffo as your Inglese, capito? Not by a mile. Sono comé bambini,
tutto! Bambini!

*They stop laughing. A silence. Steve calms himself*

Right. OK. Ancora. This is not a fork, this is a spoon. Is this a spoon?
No, this is a knife.

SCENE 2

*The staff rest room*

*The Lights come up on the upstage scene appearing in daylight*

*Music of a street organ swells*

*Steve moves into the set and starts an overhead fan by a switch beside the door, goes for some air at the window, listens to the organ, takes banknotes from his pocket and floats them down, smiling and waving*

*Gennaro Manetti, 30, enters, sees the fan and turns it off*

**Gennaro**  Signor Flowers.
**Steve**  Signor Manetti.
**Gennaro**  Prego. Mi scuso per non aver fatto visita alla sua prima lezione / ma avere da fare.
**Steve**  Scusi. Momento. Signor. Non capisco Italiano. Not yet anyway. Parlo poco pochissimo.
**Gennaro**  No. I forget. Sorry. I say: excuse me that I do not visit your first class. I was busy. (*He crosses irritably to the window; calling aggressively*) Grazie tante. Ma adesso basta, eh? (*He shuts the window*)

*The music reduces from forte to piano*

Mi dica. Dunque. What have you said to this class?
**Steve**  Well, what I'm supposed to: "this is a spoon, a fork, a knife. / Is this a spoon —— "
**Gennaro**  You did not insult them?
**Steve**  Insult them?
**Gennaro**  You consider them stupid?
**Steve**  Average.
**Gennaro**  You didn't call them stupid?
**Steve**  I said they were behaving like children. Comé bambini. Which they were.

*Gennaro walks away, shaking his head, evidently worried*

**Gennaro**  One thing you must never say to a group of Italian boys and girls.
**Steve**  Young men and women.

**Gennaro**  Teenagers, not perhaps one year after school, trying hard to be grown-up in the adult language school, big and strong and beautiful for each other. Then comes this English *professore*, very serious, very stern.

**Steve**  Stern? Me?

**Gennaro**  To them a figure of authority.

**Steve**  That's not how they've been acting. More like I'm a figure of fun. Capito? Mi prendono per un culo? You say that?

**Gennaro**  Not with ladies present, no. They take you for an arsehole?

**Steve**  Too strong? I learnt it from the professor of Latin you gave me. I guess someone who's used to Ovid and Plautus wouldn't think arsehole much to write home about.

**Gennaro**  To write home ...?

**Steve**  Of no consequence. Trivial, footling.

**Gennaro**  Let me speak as an Italian. You destroyed their *bella figura*. You know what this means to say?

**Steve**  Their fine face.

**Gennaro**  How they look to their friends. These are not babies. Not children / in a school.

**Steve**  Well, sorry. First words that / came to me.

**Gennaro**  They refuse to be taught by you again. I must ask Milan to transfer you. To Torino or Napoli.

**Steve**  Oh ... but I only got here two days ago.

**Gennaro**  We have anyway too many English teachers.

**Steve**  Please, don't tell Milan. I'll apologize. I'll eat humble pie.

**Gennaro**  Eat what?

**Steve**  Shit. Merda. Whatever.

**Gennaro**  Too late. Sorry. They won't speak with you.

**Steve**  They don't have to. Only listen while I speak to *them*.

**Gennaro**  I have persuaded them to stay as students but only if they are taught by one of the ladies. Whoever pays the piper calls the tune. It's correct?

**Steve**  *Too* correct. Listen, please. At home I've only taught in state schools. Non-paying pupils. Not used to volunteers. I'll change. Please let me stay. I've fallen in love.

**Gennaro**  (*alarmed*) Not with a student? È vietato. Verboten. Not allowed.

**Steve**  No. With Florence! The Florentines. I've always wanted to come, ever since I read Forster. Listen: (*finding a page in "A Room With A View" from the table*) "Someone who goes to Italy to study Giotto ... the corruption of the Papacy ... may come back remembering nothing but the blue sky and the men and women who live under it."

*Moved, Gennaro turns away to compose himself*

**Gennaro**  Beautiful. Captain Hornblower said this?
**Steve**  Not Forrester. *Forster.* It's from a novel called *A Room With A View*, set in Florence. About nineteen-o-five. The city's changed a bit in fifty years. No trams or horses.
**Gennaro**  More Americans. Can I lend it?
**Steve**  Borrow it by all means.
**Gennaro**  I am happy you love my native city. But ... I can do nothing. It would be closing the stable door after the horse has bolted. Have you another class today?
**Steve**  Two this evening. At seven and nine.
**Gennaro**  I'll give them to someone else. What can I do? Also they need English teachers in Napoli. (*He gestures "hot" and opens the window*)

*The volume of the music increases. Gennaro listens*

Rossini must turn in his grave. You say that?
**Steve**  You could. But I like it. When you throw some lire, the boy catches and the monkey raises his velvet cap.
**Gennaro**  Eat-a da ice-a-cream, da macaroni? Sing-a di Neapolitan love-songs? Arrividerci Roma? Chico Marx? You think this is Italian culture?
**Steve**  Part of it ... (*Pointing at the view through window*) And Giotto's campanile, Brunelleschi's dome, motor-scooters ... trousers so tight you can't put them on over your winkle-pickers ... narrow ties ... Gaggia machines, Gina Lollobrigida ...
**Gennaro**  Culture is also boiled cabbage, yes?
**Steve**  D'you reckon?
**Gennaro**  Not me, no. T.S. Eliot.
**Steve**  Ah. An American's view of pre-war England. Not far out actually. I prefer pizza. So would everyone if they got the chance. An Italian secret. Like espresso coffee. And those girls, aren't they beautiful! Ten Lollobrigidas facing me in one class.
**Gennaro**  Do not presume their brains will equal their beauty. You will find there is — comé si dice? — Nothing up here? Intelligence in a wife would be a matter of shame for their men. Wives must be beautiful and stupid. For company an Italian man prefers men. In England the women are clever, yes? But not beautiful.
**Steve**  Some are beautiful. Some stupid.
**Gennaro**  You will learn what stupid means when you know Italian girls better. But of course you must not.
**Steve**  Not what?
**Gennaro**  Know them better.

*Peggy Carmichael enters: 30ish, with a bright expression and eager manner; relentless smile. She wears tinted glasses and her long hair has often to be thrown back from her face. She has a large shoulder-bag and sun hat and too perfect Italian. Seeing the men, she removes the glasses*

**Peggy** Buongiorno, Gennaro. Sta bene?

**Gennaro** Buongiorno, Signorina. Mr Flowers, Miss Carmichael ——

**Peggy** Peggy.

**Steve** Steve.

**Gennaro** You must take Mr Flowers' lessons tonight. How far did you get with this class?

**Steve** Knife, fork, spoon. This is, is this, *what* is this, no / this is not.

**Gennaro** Too fast.

**Steve** (*amazed*) Too *fast*?

**Gennaro** Much too fast. That's lessons one to three in one session. You must not show the knife until session two. In the first hour speak only of forks and spoons. The direct method is slow at first. Like a baby learns. Mama. Papa. Spoon. Fork. Slow but sure, yes? And later prestissimo. (*He makes a machine-gun sound*)

**Steve** Like Rossini. A Rossini overture.

**Peggy** Signor Crescendo.

**Gennaro** Ecco! Accelerando. Debo andare. Must go.

*Gennaro goes*

*Peggy speaks as if to him, after he's gone*

**Peggy** God forbid we should delay you a moment longer than you can possibly spare. (*She turns on the fan*) Pathetic. A child. Like all Italians. Very sweet, very charming, molto simpatico, capisce? But shallow. Fickle. (*Singing*) "L'uomo é mobile." (*Speaking*) It's the fault of their mothers. And their wives. They're not expected to grow up ... or be responsible for their actions. A woman to them is Madonna or Magdalene. Saint or strumpet. Intelligence scares them stiff. No. Scares them limp. If you follow me? (*She laughs at her risqué joke*)

**Steve** Good-looking though.

**Peggy** Good looks don't rate that highly with me. I much prefer a man to be serious. I enjoy discussions, not this endless bottom-pinching of the Italian so-called male. So why does he say I must take your classes?

**Steve** I've got the sack.

**Peggy** You've hardly arrived.

*Steve shrugs and listens at the window. Peggy offers him cigarettes*

D'you use these?

**Steve** When I can afford them. All I can offer *you* is a light. A fiammifero? Great word.

*He takes one, strikes a match and lights their cigarettes. She steadies his hand with hers and examines it*

**Peggy** Fine hands. Are you a musician?

**Steve** Used to play washboard with a skiffle group. I sing a bit. But no ...

*Peggy lets go of his hand but won't take back the cigarettes*

**Peggy** Keep them. Everyone's skint when they first arrive.

**Steve** Well, thanks. The rail fare from London to Milan then Milan to here just about cleaned me out. Till we're paid, it's minestrone for lunch.

**Peggy** They say slavery's been abolished. But not with Lingua Franca. A bare living wage and we're on call six days a week, twelve hours a day.

**Steve** Not me. I only agreed eight classes a day.

**Peggy** Aah, but did they specify *which* eight hours? They can have us spooning and forking any hour from breakfast to bedtime. For no extra pay. Which is why it's unlikely you'll be sacked. White slaves aren't that thick on the ground these days. (*She opens some buttons on her blouse, leans back against the table and fans her neck and breasts with a book*) So: did you make a pass at a girl student? Shame we didn't meet sooner, I could have warned you. They go straight to the principal. If you're lucky. Worse if they go to the family. You may think you're young but to them you're middle-aged. A professore. Confine yourself to cutlery. And later stationery. "Is this a pen?"

**Steve** Do they ever learn, going this slow?

**Peggy** The longer they take, the more they pay. This is not the dreaming spires, Steve, it's the market place. But not quite a knocking-shop, as you seem to have assumed.

**Steve** Honest, Guv, I never laid a hand on any of them.

**Peggy** No need. A word's enough, an admiring glance, especially from a foreigner. Above all, an Englishman. They think we're all sex-maniacs and murderers like that man Christie with the bombetta. Bowler hat. Jack the Ripper. Rapists. Voracious Jezebels. (*She makes flamboyant sexual gestures at him*) But, of course, English is what they all want to learn. Well, American. They all apply for American. They're shocked to hear there's no such animal.

*The music of the street organ fades*

**Steve** The organ's moved on. I love it here. Can *you* help me change Signor Manetti's mind?

**Peggy** Me? Change Gennaro? You really have no idea how very droll that is, have you? (*She laughs*)

*Steve turns to look at her*

SCENE 3

*A classroom*

*The stage is in darkness with a spotlight on Signora Irena Brentano, seated, giving a private lesson. 50, once a beauty, now handsome, in rather exotic fabrics, beads and jewellery, a headscarf, hair ballerina style. Accented speech*

**Irena** ... Well, I know you well enough now, Signora, to confess that my English accent isn't perfect. I'm after all a Russian Jew who married an Italian. It's not quite honest of Lingua Franca to pass me off as English. Like others here who may be Australian, Canadian, German, Dutch, even Indian. Because it's now the world language, it's spoken in so many different ways. Even the natives don't speak it well — Cockneys, Irish, Scotch, Welsh. If you want a good accent to copy, ask for Miss Carmichael. Or Mr Flowers. Like all the new arrivals, he stayed last night on my balcony. It's clever of Signor Manetti always to offer the best view first, over the city from my villa beyond the Arno. They fall in love with it, as I did. This young man speaks like you hear on BBC. Just as Florentine's the best Italian. Shall I arrange some lessons with him before your holiday in London? ... Not that you really need it. You've come a long way from the forks and spoons. How wise you were to pay to be a class of one. The others would have held you back, in the wrong-headed assumption of Equality. Communism, which I hasten to add I ardently believed in once myself.

*A handbell rings*

Ecco! Ciao, Signora. Arrivederla. Alla prossima.

*Irena turns into the staff rest room as the lights change*

SCENE 4

*The staff rest room*

*The Lights come up on Steve and Peggy in the staff rest room as before.*
*Peggy is sitting, marking work*

*Irena joins them*

**Peggy** Buongiorno, Signora. Una bella giornata, vero?
**Irena** Yes, very nice.

*The bell rings again. Peggy finishes marking and rises*

**Peggy** Poor Signor Valentini. Throwing his lire down the drain. Not
only a tin ear but illiterate. After my hour with him, if you're free,
Steve, I could buy you an espresso.
**Steve** I've got a class then. Shame. Thanks anyway.

*Peggy shrugs to show how little she cares*

**Peggy** Fa niente. Lunch then? Man cannot live by panino alone. See
you for lunch.

*Peggy goes with her stuff*

*Irena watches then smiles at Steve*

**Steve** So you teach English too?
**Irena** Not enough takers for Russian. Only a few Communists hoping
one day to go / to Moscow.
**Steve** I was a Communist some years back. For several years I believed
in the brotherhood of man.
**Irena** (*smiling, shaking her head*) How sweet! In the second half of the
twentieth century? Very sweet. My father was Communist. He died in
one of Stalin's purges ...
**Steve** (*smiling, acknowledging the difference*) Yeah, well, there weren't
any purges in our local branch, in Swindon. We couldn't afford to lose
anyone.

SCENE 5

*A classroom*

*The stage is in darkness, with a spotlight on Madge Fox, at the table with the cutlery. She is 45, bulky and weatherbeaten, with a strong Australian accent*

**Madge**  (*showing spoon to a class*) Was ist das? Das ist ein Löffel. Ist das ein Löffel? Ja, das ist ein Löffel. (*She holds up a fork*) Ist das ein Löffel? Nein, das ist ein Gabel. Was ist das? Das ist ein — che cosa, Giovanni? Gabel, ja! Und das? (*She holds up a knife*) Das ist ein Messer. OK. Round the class. Leonardo — was ist das?

*The bell rings. She's obviously relieved*

Oh, already? Next time you'll be having a real German teacher. Glad tidings all round, right? ... Oh, for Chrissake, those who understand English explain it to the others.

*Madge turns into the staff rest room*

SCENE 6

*The staff rest room*

*The Lights come up on Madge entering the room where Steve is alone, lighting one of Peggy's cigarettes. From the open window, the snarling of Vespas and blaring loudspeaker announcements can be heard*

**Madge**  Last time I take a German class. That bloody lingo says a lot about the nation that speaks it, don't you think? Hang about — you're not the new Kraut teacher, by any chance?
**Steve**  Steven Flowers. English.
**Madge**  (*shaking hands*) Madge Fox. Beg your pardon. No offence, calling you a Kraut. Shut the finestra, Steve, for Chrissake, cut out that bloody row.

*Steve shuts the window. The noise from the window decreases. There's the sound of many Italian voices as the students change classes in the hall*

No one with a sense of humour could get through a sentence without busting out laughing. Whenever I hear of Hynies, I remember old Frau Mauser. I'm talking about the Lisbon branch. Reckoned all the men were in love with her. Owned up to forty but she won't see fifty again.

*Irena comes from the washroom and checks her face in a pocket glass*

Well, she could never get enough fellers. The body wasn't bad but the face! That moustache. Well, let's be honest, beard!

**Irena**  Oh, Madge, not this again?

**Madge**  Steve hasn't heard it, have you?

**Irena**  Don't listen, Steven.

**Madge**  S'all right for you, you were never *in* the Lisbon branch. Never knew old Mauser. Finished me when I saw her without her teeth during the earthquake. (*She takes out a cigarette*)

*Steve lights the cigarette for her*

I nearly fell out of bed myself when it started. Middle of the bloody night, the whole bloody place shaking. We all knew one had destroyed the city way back when, so everyone was in the street in what they slept in, mostly a dab of eau-de-cologne. Not a pretty sight, believe me.

*Jestin Overton enters by the main door; 65, benign, dapper, carrying an old school satchel crammed with personal items*

**Jestin**  Good morning, ladies. More than good. Miraculous. Sir? Jestin Overton. How are you?

**Steve**  Steven Flowers.

**Irena**  Befriend him, Steven. A good deed in a naughty world.

**Jestin**  Nothing of the sort, Irena. A mere human.

*Another ring of the bell*

*Irena goes*

**Madge**  Well, old Mauser ran downstairs so sharp she forgot to put her choppers in. Christ, she give me a worse shock than the quake itself. Right off the bloody Richter Scale. But, here's the point, Steve, beard or no, teeth in or out, she always had a nice young feller on the go. And

why? Free bloody lessons up in her room. I wonder if Lingua Franca
ever found out they'd been pimping for her for fifteen bloody years.

**Jestin** Miss Fox, you'll never go to heaven.

**Madge** How's that, my old love?

**Jestin** Repeating such untruths. In front of this young man, who doesn't
know your wicked tongue.

**Madge** He'll take us as he finds us, eh, Steve? As for heaven, d'you
reckon you've booked your passage?

**Jestin** Let him that is without sin cast the first stone. In any case, there's
no such place, more's the pity.

*Gennaro looks in at the main door*

**Gennaro** Miss Fox, Signor Bargellini is asking for you.

**Madge** Bloody sauce. Doesn't show up for bloody weeks then he's
champing at the bloody bit.

**Gennaro** He has paid for the course. You should await him in the
classroom, whether he comes or not.

**Madge** I've hardly drawn breath since the Kraut lesson, which by rights
I shouldn't have to take.

**Gennaro** The new German teacher will come tomorrow. Now hurry,
please. Is Signor Bargellini doing well?

**Madge** Who? Oh. My next one? He'll never speak-a da-Ingleesh if he
tries for a bloody millennium.

*Madge starts collecting cutlery, pens and a text book*

*Gennaro goes*

**Jestin** So, young sir, you are one of the chosen?

**Steve** Jewish, d'you mean? No.

**Jestin** No, being here in Florence for the first time. How I envy you!
I said there's no heaven but this is as near as we can get on earth.
And yet — this morning — coming from my lodgings — I happened
upon the most beautiful spectacle I've yet seen in this city crammed
with beauty. Not a fountain in the Boboli Gardens, not a Della Robbia
medallion of some chubby choirboy, not even Mussolini's wonderful
railway station ... but a girl! Yes! A child sitting on a wall on the
Lungarno, her face shimmering in sunlight reflected from the water. I
was enchanted. I threw her a kiss.

**Madge** She'd have preferred lire.

*Madge has gathered her stuff and goes to class*

**Jestin** That would hardly have been proper. As I walked away, I
realized it was near the spot where legend claims Dante first set eyes
on Beatrice. And loved her ever after.

**Steve** How old was she?

**Jestin** Nine, I believe, the same as Dante.

**Steve** No, not Beatrice, this girl you saw?

**Jestin** Oh — perhaps fourteen? At my age a certain gallantry's allowed,
even expected. At yours better not even start.

**Steve** So I've been told.

**Jestin** Good advice. For a single man as young as you.


SCENE 7

*A classroom*

*The stage is in darkness. Jestin moves down to sit at the teacher's desk.
A spotlight comes up on him. He addresses the audience, as a single
student*

No, I've never married. Since you ask, Signora. Must seem odd to
an Italian wife and mother. So think of one of your priests. Though
celibate, I was never drawn to the cloth, finding organized religion
anathema, opposed to all I apprehend of God. I've never been able
to treat brutally any living creature I find beautiful. It's not ethics so
much as *aes*thetics. I'm not going too fast, Signora? Tend to forget it's
only a few months since you got cracking with the spoons and forks ...
got *started*, yes.

*He listens to a question we don't hear*

No, I'm often told physical love isn't always harmful or hurtful.
People clearly *do* find it enjoyable to do this — thing — to one
another, though it's still an act of violence, often committed against
the wish of one of the parties ... and I can neither grant nor assume
that right. We hardly need more births, God knows. I've lived through
the two most thoroughgoing massacres in history ... Yet here we are in
danger of another, which would be the last. Too many of us and more
every minute. Rats in a cage. So your Pope and I have done our tiny
good deed by remaining celibate. Which he then cancels by blessing
the breeders, the rams, the tuppers fertilizing the ewes with yet more
unnecessary lambs.

SCENE 8

*A classroom*

*Spotlight on Peggy sitting at a table, taking a private lesson*

**Peggy**  You ask about London, Signora. As a tourist for a week or two you would have a pleasant and interesting visit. The city has as rich a history as any European capital. Many of its monuments have survived the world war. But — if as a student you stay longer, you'll find its people broken in spirit, exhausted by shortages, wondering when the fruits of victory will be coming off ration. You too may find yourself alone and neglected, desperate for a kind word from someone. It's a great heartless place, like its tower, stony and cruel. Why d'you think I left it? Why do so many of us come south to find a warmer climate, kinder people? I hope you won't end as I did, walking out at night through busy streets, a solitary girl, half afraid of strangers, half longing for their company. It may not happen. I just thought I should warn you it could.

SCENE 9

*A classroom*

*Spotlight on Steve sitting at the other table, smoking*

**Steve**  Not London, no. I was born and brought up in Swindon. Wiltshire. Well, *a* Wiltshire. Not the same one as Salisbury Cathedral and Stonehenge and the White Horse ... just rows of houses put up for the men who built the railways a century ago. When I saw my parents doing what their parents had done, I buggered off ... ah, left. One thing Swindon did have: trains to London. Am I going too fast, Professore? ... I know you want to hear colloquial speech but are you understanding? ... Yes, it's your money. Fair enough. OK ...

*The bell sounds*

*Black-out*

SCENE 10

*A classroom*

*A spotlight comes up on Jestin, seated*

**Jestin** Ah. The tocsin. The parting bell. I hope our little chats have been
some use. I'm supposed to recruit you for another course but truly I
think you'd be wasting your money. You'll easily pick up all you need
from the foreigners who come to stay at the hotel you're buying here.
Good luck, Signora. Arrivederci. Ciao.

*He offers his hand to shake*

*Black-out*

*The sound of student chatter as the classes change*

SCENE 11

*The staff rest room*

*The Lights come up on Peggy, without glasses, looking in a hand
mirror*

*Steve comes in with his text books*

*Peggy turns*

**Peggy** All done for the morning?
**Steve** Till four o'clock.
**Peggy** Good. Me too.
**Steve** Manetti passed this Italian professor to me. Teaches classics at
university. Too proud to speak English in a bad accent but understands
well and likes to listen.
**Peggy** You look the sort who usually falls on your feet.
**Steve** D'you know what Macaronic means? Macaronic verse?

*He takes a "Dictionary of Quotations" from the bookcase*

**Peggy** Isn't it a sort-of medley of Latin and English?

**Steve**  Right. Clever girl. I'd never heard of it till the professor told me. A poetic pidgin. Yes. Look. Doctor Johnson said — "Macaronic, a confused mixture of different languages."
**Peggy**  Assorted pasta.
**Steve**  Linguistic linguine.
**Peggy**  Dandies used it when they went on the Grand Tour. Thus Yankee Doodle stuck a feather in his cap and was called Macaroni. Ecco!
**Steve**  That a fact? Well, all this talk of pasta reminds me, I'm famished. What I miss most about home is the Full English.
**Peggy**  Midday I usually go to a tavola calda. Not too dear and molto gustosa.
**Steve**  I'll have to manage with a slice of pizza on the street.
**Peggy**  You must eat. Big boy like you.
**Steve**  I like pizza. Never tasted it before. The first café sells it in London will make a pile.
**Peggy**  The English will never eat foreign food. Not enough of them anyway. Certainly not the NBs.
**Steve**  The what?
**Peggy**  No Backgrounds. (*She turns away*)

*Steve makes a face at her*

**Steve**  Anyway, till payday I couldn't / pay you back —
**Peggy**  Didn't I say? My treat.
**Steve**  No, I already owe / you the money you —
**Peggy**  And I already told you, fa niente. My pleasure. È pronto lei?
**Steve**  Hang on.

*Steve goes into the washroom*

*Peggy does her face in the glass*

*Jestin opens the main door and looks about*

**Jestin**  I was looking for the new boy. Steven?

*Peggy crosses to block his way in*

**Peggy**  (*quietly*) He went out for a pizza. If you hurry you might catch him. Via Campidoglio.

*Jestin nods and goes*

*Peggy goes to the washroom door*

(*Calling*) By the way, did I see you talking to the girl students on the landing? Only that's absolutely vietato. Taboo. Not to say terribly dangerous. So easy for them to get the wrong idea. Not only the girls but their families and boyfriends and, believe me, that way there be dragons.

*Steve comes back, combing his hair with a wet comb*

**Steve** There be what?
**Peggy** Danger. You don't mind my warning you?
**Steve** I'm here to pick up Italian.
**Peggy** But not Italians. Italiane. Feminine plural. That's what they'll *think*. They always assume the worst. One day her brothers will be in that corridor to ask your intentions. And if they're not honourable — which means marriage ——
**Steve** Oh no, come on ——
**Peggy** I'm serious — you may very well finish with a knife in your back floating in the Arno.
**Steve** As in, "This is a knife"? As in coltello?
**Peggy** As in daga.

*She grabs one of the knives among the assorted cutlery and mimes sticking it into him, with almost too much relish, then laughs*

Capito? I just thought you should be warned.

*Steve puts on a hat with a raccoon's tail hanging behind*

Oh! A Davy Crockett hat!
**Steve** Right first time. They've just gone out in England but here it still makes the heads turn.
**Peggy** You have been warned, va bene?

*She puts on dark glasses and makes for the main door, then has to search with her hand for the door-knob. Steve opens it for her and smiles*

*Steve follows Peggy out*

SCENE 12

*The staff rest room*

*There is night lighting on the room, the tower and cathedral dome lit against a black sky. The window is open with sound from the street as before*

*Heidi, 22, blonde hair done up into neat braids, severe demeanour, is standing behind the table, showing cutlery. Gennaro sits on the far side, watching, as yet unseen*

**Heidi** Was ist das? Das ist ein Löffel. Das ist ein Gabel. Ist es ein Gabel? Ja, es ist ein Gabel. E basta, sì? Troppo di quello.

*She puts the cutlery aside*

Das ist (*touching her head*) der Kopf ... (*touching her ear*) das Ohr ... (*touching her face*) das Gesicht ... Die Augen, die Nase, der Mund, die Lippe, das Haar ...

*She releases one plait, which falls to its full length; she puts out her tongue and moves it from side to side*

Die Zunge ... (*touching her neck*) Der Hals, (*touching her shoulders*) Die Schulter, (*undoing two buttons of her shirt*) Die Brust ... Die Taille ... Der Schenkel ...

*She puts her hands on her hips, runs them downward and raises her skirt*

Das Knie, das Bein, der Fuss, die Zehen ...

*She comes downstage and sits on the table. She slips off one shoe, which falls to the floor; then the other; her leg and feet bare, toenails painted. Gennaro moves towards her*

**Gennaro** You go too far.
**Heidi** Too far?
**Gennaro** Too fast. Not speaking German, like the class, I don't think I'd remember beyond your lips ... maybe your tongue ... die Zunge? ...
**Heidi** This is to tell them what's to come. Parts of the body may take three weeks. I think they like it more than forks and spoons, don't you?

**Gennaro** Jawohl, bestimmt! Only don't forget they're simple people. Not educated. Going to do low-class jobs in the factories of Stuttgart, the kitchens of Munich.
**Heidi** My home town. Munchen.
**Gennaro** I only mean don't expect they can run before they walk. More slow. Lentamente. (*He goes on one knee, picks up Heidi's shoe, replaces it on her foot and caresses her leg*)

*Heidi stands and moves to shut the window. The street sounds reduce*

**Heidi** Hey listen, isn't it great I now have mein phut-phut?

*Gennaro looks confused*

Mein Vespa scooter. It follows me from Napoli by train. Now who cares this room you found me is so far on Lungarno Amerigo Vespucci? I'm there in two shakes.
**Gennaro** It's a little way out but the landlady, she's very diplomatic. All day she plays Canasta with her friends, doesn't notice who comes, who goes. Also doesn't know my wife and children / so can't —
**Heidi** (*putting her hands on her ears, at the window*) D'you think I want to hear about your little Signora, your bambini? Your happy family? Please, when you're with me, don't. I know we haven't long met / but already —
**Gennaro** Cara ...
**Heidi** I can't wait to move there. It's all right now with the old Russian lady but you couldn't very well come visit me there, I think.
**Gennaro** No, no. Irena knows my wife, she —

*Heidi puts her hands on her ears again. Gennaro stops*

**Heidi** When will the Englishman go to Napoli so that you can surely keep me on the staff here?
**Gennaro** Soon. After he insults this class, he makes it hard for me to keep him. Dommage! Because I like him. Molto simpatico. You've met him?
**Heidi** Nein. But I know the English, believe me. Cold, no heart. Arrogant. They think they won the war but it was the Americans. You and I, Liebchen, we know that, don't we, huh?

*Gennaro turns the key, locking the door. Heidi takes up her handbag, sits on the table again and improves her make-up looking in a glass*

Our countries were on the same side until you killed your Duce.
Without the Americans the English would never win. But now they
pay the price.

*Gennaro approaches Heidi again. Continuing to do her face, she partly
opens her legs. He kneels between her knees, kissing them*

**Gennaro**  Das Knie ... der Schenkel ...
**Heidi**  The price is giving England to the Americans. So crazy when
Hitler only wanted peace with England. He always said England could
keep her empire. This is why he invades Russia instead.

*She finishes her face, puts away her bag and raises her knees to embrace
Gennaro with her legs*

We could all have shared Africa between us. You could have Abyssinia,
like before, / and Germany could have kept Europe.
**Gennaro**  The others have all gone home. We are alone.
**Heidi**  This is why he doesn't destroy their army at Dunkirk.
**Gennaro**  Cara, no more politics.

*Heidi lies back across the table, face downstage, to the audience*

**Heidi**  You've been to England, ja? You speak so good English.
**Gennaro**  No, I haven't. Want to but can't afford.
**Heidi**  Such beautiful places they've got there. Country houses and
enormous parks and so ... But everyone so poor. Even their rich are
poor. Germany starts to get well again and all Europe wants Italian
fashions ... but the English — kaputt, finito. Triste, n'est-ce pas?
Screwed by America, ja? I was au pair for this American family in
Chelsea.
**Gennaro**  (*moving up her body*) Voglio fare l'amore con te ...
**Heidi**  Horse-paintings and Persian carpets and so. The Bechstein on
which the older child played only boogie-woogie. And only in C
Major.
**Gennaro**  Voglio chiavare, cara ...
**Heidi**  Sometimes when I was left with the baby, I'd wear the mother's
clothes. Mink coats, diamond necklace ... Sometimes a boyfriend
came and I'd play him maybe a Mozart sonata ... wearing only this
sable coat ...
**Gennaro**  Aah, fottiamo, deliziosa ——
**Heidi**  One time I asked one English boy if it didn't worry him all the
best English houses were lived in by rich Jews? One other time I was

kidding, you know, and asked if *he'd* ever be able to dress me in mink
... or if I'd have to find myself a nice little Jewish sugar-daddy.

*Gennaro stops making love*

Hey, listen, I hope you don't think Heidi's just some silly little girl
with no ideas in her head?

*Gennaro stands and moves away. Heidi remains. He turns on the harsh
overhead light*

**Gennaro**  Come, I must be home. It's late.
**Heidi**  Cosa? Ma perché, caro? Che succede?
**Gennaro**  Niente. Time to go.
**Heidi**  (*trying to embrace him*) Non ho capito, Liebchen.
**Gennaro**  (*moving away, unlocking the door and holding it for her*) I
    must be home.
**Heidi**  Won't you come on mein phut-phut, show me the room?
**Gennaro**  No. Svelta, andiamo.
**Heidi**  Allora, buona notte. Dormez bien, with your little Madonna. I
    think maybe she won't sleep much tonight, è vero? Lucky girl. She
    gets from you the result of me.
**Gennaro**  (*holding the door for her*) Gute nacht, Fräulein.

*Heidi gives him a long stare, then goes past him and out*

*Gennaro slams the door after her and goes to open the window, letting
in fresh air and street sounds: scooters, voices, laughter*

Scene 13

*A classroom*

*Daylight. Madge appears at one side, taking a class*

**Madge**  All those who wanted to learn American, alzate le mani! (*She
    looks about*) Right, hands down, ears pinned back. There's no such
    lingo, capeesh? It's only English spoken badly. If you want to speak
    like a gangster or cowboy, you're in the wrong class. Here we learn
    the Queen's English. Not that she's much of a model. Talks as though
    she's got a frozen poker up her fundament. Mai hesbund end Ai ..
    No, dear, you weren't meant to capeesh. That's the more advanced
    lesson. And don't let me hear any of *you* insulting our Queen. I've

seen those slogans on the walls. *Vacca Elisabetta. Porca regina.* As a loyal subject, I won't have foreigners piss on our queen, cow or no. No, here we do the tongue that Shakespeare spake. Not that travesty spoken by Elvis the Pelvis. I take it even you, Franco, have heard of Shakespeare?

**Franco** Sure thing. *Romeo and Giulietta. Ze lahvurs ov Verona. Amore, amore ...*

*Laughter from the others. Some sex-talk in Italian. Madge waits for silence*

**Madge** Finished talking smut? ... And we say Luvvers. Not lahvayrz. Say it.

**Franco** Lahvayrz.

**Madge** Terrible. Afraid you've got a tin ear, sonny. And, by the way, in English, "lovers" isn't the same as sex maniacs.

**Franco** But, Signora ——

**Madge** Signor*ina.*

**Franco** Signorina — Romeo and Giulietta, they are not Inglese but Italian teenager. *Sono molto amorosi. Sensuale. Capito?*

*Laughter and sexy sounds. Madge waits and looks at her watch*

**Madge** I get paid by the hour, not by how fast you learn. Suits me, suits Lingua Franca, because the longer you take, the more lessons you pay for, *capito,* Franco?

*Silence*

(*Going on rapidly*) You're right in a way, though. Romeo probably was like you. A cock-happy little Eyeteye. The moment he clapped eyes on Juliet he knew she'd been keeping it for the worms and before you could say knife he was up the trellis doing a spot of interior decorating.

*Pause*

See how far there is to go before you've cracked the lingo?

SCENE 14

*The staff rest room*

*Daylight. Peggy is marking books, wearing glasses; Irena is looking out from the window. They are both smoking*

*Gennaro comes in, a step or two*

**Gennaro**  Has Signor Flowers not come in yet?
**Irena**  He's got no lessons. You've fired him, haven't you?
**Gennaro**  Maybe. Maybe not.
**Irena**  I have to tell you, it seems very wrong, just for telling that class they were like babies.
**Peggy**  In England, it would be a case for unfair dismissal. We'd all be out on strike, parading with placards.
**Gennaro**  And here in Italy I should be forced to advertise for a new staff and within an hour there would be —

*Heidi comes from the washroom, brushing her long hair. During the next, she braids it again*

(*Turning to the door*) When he comes, please tell him I wish to see him.
**Peggy**  (*stopping him*) Gennaro — I must insist you have a word with him about talking to the girl students. He's unable to appreciate the danger. It could so easily bring the whole school into disrepute.

*Jestin enters, leaving the door open*

**Gennaro**  I already did.
**Peggy**  You should again. He's new. He doesn't know.
**Gennaro**  OK, OK.
**Peggy**  I mean, look! (*She lets him look into the hall*)
**Gennaro**  (*looking*) Va bene. Basta.

*Gennaro goes, shutting the door*

**Jestin**  Who doesn't know what?
**Peggy**  The new boy. Standing out there, blatantly chatting up those girls.
**Jestin**  Practising his basic Italian. I heard him.
**Peggy**  "Sono innamorato di lei, carissima"? "Vuole dormire con me, signorina?"

*Jestin shakes his head. Peggy approaches Heidi*

Heidi, it's something you should be warned about too —
**Heidi** Ja? Cosa c'é?
**Peggy** If you haven't been in Italy long. Their attitudes to the opposite sex.
**Heidi** Hey, listen, I've been three months in Naples. Before that, Milan, London, Brussels ...
**Peggy** Then you already know what our poor baby of a principal never seems to learn.

*Behind Peggy, Jestin and Irena are amused*

He may be a husband and father of two sons but he's never grown up, never will. Claims he enjoys discussions with a mature woman-friend but let her make clear she's not the staff tart, the town pump, which they assume all foreign girls are, merely hint she might make a dent in his masculine ego, he's off home like a scalded cat.

*Heidi considers this. Jestin approaches her*

**Jestin** We haven't met. Jestin Overton. I've been away for a few days.
**Heidi** Heidi Schumann. How d'you do.
**Jestin** Never better, thank you, my dear. I hope you learn to love Florence as I do. If I may say so, your very presence has added to its charms, its legendary beauty.
**Heidi** Danke schön.
**Jestin** Doubly welcome, of course, as we can none of us wait to relinquish our German classes. I've heard it said it's the language they speak in heaven but to my ears it sounds somewhat harsh. With respect.
**Heidi** Harsh? Goethe, Schiller, Heine, Brecht?
**Jestin** I haven't read the originals. And I hardly speak a word.
**Irena** Nor of any other language. Five years here you still talk to everyone in English.
**Jestin** The lingua franca of our age. Time's coming when there'll only be different dialects of English.
**Heidi** Only because of the Americans, not having one of their own.

*The bell rings*

Ah, another class begins?
**Irena** Ends. The next begins with the second bell.

*Steve enters, wearing dark glasses, smoking, looking smart*

**Peggy** The wanderer returns. Did Gennaro speak to you?
**Steve** *Frowned* at me.
**Peggy** (*to the rest of them, laughing*) What did I tell you? A hopeless child.
**Steve** What is it now?
**Peggy** I assume you *want* to finish up being scraped off the pavement below the campanile? That was your intention all along? See Firenze and die?

*Steve sees Heidi*

**Irena** (*to Peggy*) Steady, my dear.
**Steve** Steve Flowers.
**Heidi** Heidi Schumann.

*The bell rings*

Scusi.

*Heidi leaves, passing close by Steve, on the way to class*

*Steve checks the timetable*

**Jestin** So. D'you have a class now?
**Steve** Not till two. Came in to pick up mail.
**Jestin** Then shall we buy a sandwich and spend half an hour with Michelangelo's *Pietà* in the Duomo?
**Peggy** I thought we'd go to a tavola calda as usual, Steve. Just a snack, as we're eating at my place tonight.
**Jestin** I love the way local women use the cathedral as a short cut, crossing from one door to the other with their shopping bags, a quick genuflection as they pass the altar. The house of God / is their house too.
**Peggy** That's what you *said*. A light lunch?
**Jestin** Don't let me interfere with / any previous arrangement ——
**Steve** Thing is, I promised Jestin yesterday to go / some time and look at ——
**Peggy** (*shrugging, unnaturally bright*) Fa niente. It really makes no odds to me where we go. But you know, don't you, that Michelangelo never finished the *Pietà* and the Madonna figure is inferior work by a student?
**Jestin** I didn't, no, and somehow feel none the better now I do.

**Peggy** Allora, arrivederla. See you in an hour then.

*Peggy goes to her class*

**Steve** Come on, Jestin. Let's go on.
**Jestin** Oh, that's hardly considerate.
**Steve** We didn't invite her.
**Jestin** But if she's lonely enough to invite herself, shouldn't we recognize that need and wait?

*Madge comes from class*

**Madge** The new Kraut seems all right considering, but it's no dice, I can't abide the buggers. The very sound of their voices gives me hives.
**Irena** They can't expect the world to love them.
**Jestin** All the more reason we should try.
**Irena** I'm a Russian Jew who married an anti-Fascist Italian. How d'you *expect* me to feel?
**Jestin** You can't hold that child responsible for all that. She wasn't even born when the Nazis came to power. It would be like blaming *me* for the slave trade. Or as though Madge hadn't forgiven us British for transportation, Botany Bay, all that?
**Madge** You reckon we have?
**Jestin** Dear ladies. Bless my soul! Here's the world hovering on the brink. It's a matter of love or death. If we in this room can't embrace one another without fear, what hope for the great big world out there?
**Steve** Embrace, OK. But love or die? That's too tough on those who can't.
**Jestin** Can't?
**Steve** Love.
**Jestin** To love is natural. It's only that we're taught not to.
**Steve** Or vice versa. Love's a gift not everyone has.

*Jestin goes to the washroom*

Is he for real?
**Irena** Real?
**Steve** Or too good to be true?
**Irena** Don't you think he's right? We must learn to be Europeans. Forgive and forget is our only hope.
**Madge** You'll have to excuse me if I draw the line at the Master Race.
**Irena** If I'm honest, the Germans weren't any more brutal here than the English.

**Madge**  To you? Why would they be? You were allies. Well, not you personally, love, but the real Eyeteyes.
**Steve**  Did you know, during the war, Italians were more popular in England than Americans?
**Madge**  Only because they always ran away.
**Irena**  My husband never ran from anyone. He fought Fascism all his life. How was *your* war, Madge?
**Madge**  We had one of our own. Case you'd forgot. Against the Nips. Who'd have thought I'd end up teaching the bastards to parlay English? Queer bloody world, ain't it?

*Black-out*

*Irena moves to sit at one of the tables*

SCENE 15

*A classroom*

*Spotlight on Irena*

**Irena**  (*teaching*) They came through here one after another. The Germans fired their guns at the English so the English had to fire their guns back. Bang-bang. Pop-pop. They kept a move apart, as in a game. The Allied Tommies used a Ghirlandaio as a darts-board ... and a bust of Dante for a pisspot. Both lots of officers took care not to destroy the architecture, meaning they demolished the bridge of Santa Trinità and left us this silly Ponte Vecchio ... this bit of postcard kitsch for the tourists. The Germans warned the old people to leave their homes before they blew them up. But many were too frightened to understand and hid in the cellars or attics. And the soldiers didn't have time to search and blew the houses to smithereens with them inside ... (*Responding to a question*) Smithereens? Frammenti. Small pieces. The ones who got out had nowhere to go. They wandered like sleepwalkers between two armies shelling the town. My cowsheds on Via Belvedere crammed with refugees. It was easy finding rooms for the English, just vacated by the Germans. Then came knocking at the door this young British trooper, covered with those pretty leaves they used to wear, like some dryad from Botticelli's *Primavera* in the Uffizi. I said, "I'll show you your room." No, he said, he'd come about signals being made from my house. I could hardly understand his accent, poor boy, I think from Somerset. (*She listens again*) No.

Some*rset*. Some*rsault* vuole dire "capriola". It is in the West. They
walked me through the pouring rain. They were very nice, gave me a
cape to keep my hair dry. The sinister signallers turned out to be the
old refugees from town answering the call of nature. "Oh but, Signora,
I was so careful with the lamp."

*The bell rings. Irena makes an apologetic gesture*

I'm sorry. Did I go too fast? Ha capito? Bene. Have a good vacation in
England. I hope they don't say you speak with a Russian accent.

*Black-out*


SCENE 16

*A classroom*

*Spotlight on Madge showing an apple*

**Madge**  (*in a heavily Australian accent*) C'est une pomme. Est-ce-que
c'est une pomme? Oui, c'est une pomme. (*She changes the apple for
a banana*) Eh voilà! Est-ce-que ceci s'appelle une pomme? Non, c'est
une banane. Alors, mademoiselle, preferez-vous une pomme ou une
banane?
**Female Student** (*fluently*) Je prefère une banane qu'une pomme. Mais
sans doute une pomme mange bien aussi. On dit: chacun à son goût,
oui?

*Madge stares at the student for some moments*

*The bell rings*

**Madge**  (*smiling with evident relief*) Ah, déjà? Alors. Au revoir, chaps
and chapesses. Prochaine fois.

SCENE 17

*The staff rest room*

*The Lights come up on Irena, Jestin and Peggy coming from their classes. Madge turns to join them*

**Madge** Irena, did you say the new Kraut can do French as well?

**Irena** French, German, English, Italian. Even Spanish at a pinch, she tells me.

**Madge** She'd better get her skates on then, 'cos I can't hold this class at lesson four much longer. They're way ahead of me.

**Irena** She leaves my house today. Gennaro's found her a room.

**Peggy** Not the one along Lungarno Vespucci? So she's another of his five-minute wonders? God, how sad! Almost funny, if it weren't so pathetic.

**Jestin** Very pretty little thing. A true Rhinemaiden. They are pretty, the Teutons. You can almost see why they went for all those demented notions about racial purity.

**Peggy** And Peter Pan's installed her in his usual love nest.

**Irena** I hope he isn't serious. A married man can't afford to fall for that heady mixture of Wagnerian idealism and Prussian methodology.

**Jestin** If I ever listened to you ladies I should blush from morn till night at your scurrilous tales. Gennaro seemed to me almost cool to her.

*Steve enters with a book and cutlery. He throws them down*

**Irena** I can tell you she's not here for the beauties of Florence. The two nights she was with me she never gave the city a glance. Just kept on about her Vespa scooter. "Ach, ven I get mein phut-phut, zen I vill see ze town."

**Jestin** I've an hour before my next, so, Steven, how about a sandwich in Santa Croce, wait for a tourist to spend some lire lighting up the Giotto frescoes?

**Steve** It's where old Lucy Honeychurch met that awful prick of a vicar.

**Irena** Steven, really!

**Steve** Scusi.

**Jestin** We're doing a Stations of the Cross of the scenes in Forster's novel.

**Steve** OK. A panone. Why not?

**Peggy** If you can wait till one, I could come with you but I've got this class at twelve.

**Steve** Oh. Shame.

**Peggy** Will you be back afterwards, Steve?

**Steve** Not till evening.

**Peggy** When, don't forget, you're due at my place for a bite. As soon as you can make it.

**Steve** Va bene. A stasera. Ciao. (*He opens the main door*)

*Heidi enters, dressed Italian — loose sweater, short skirt, high-heeled sandals, long loose hair, dark glasses*

*Steve hovers*

**Heidi** Those silly boys on the street. They're as bad here as in Napoli. As soon as they see you on a phut-phut, they think they can start pinching your buttocks and so.

**Peggy** You'll need your scooter to reach that room he's put you in. Quite a trek.

**Heidi** Listen, he says now it isn't free after all. Someone else takes it. So I have nowhere. (*To Irena*) Perhaps, Signora, you won't mind if I stay another night?

**Irena** Mi dispiace, no, I have a relative coming.

**Jestin** Ready, Steven?

*Jestin leaves*

*Steve lingers then follows Jestin*

**Peggy** There's a divan in mine. You're welcome till you find / somewhere of your own ——

**Heidi** Cela m'est égal. So just for a night or so, ja?

**Peggy** Sara benvenuto molto.

**Heidi** Danke schön. Allora — je dois pee-pee.

*Heidi leaves by the washroom door*

*The bell rings*

**Madge** (*getting up*) Rather you than me. Inside a day she'll have taken over. You'll be asking when you can use your own karsi. Nearly as bad as the Nipponese.

**Peggy** That shows an unforgiving spirit.

*Madge shrugs and exits*

Still dwelling on the war. How shall we ever agree to live together on this planet with only these old animosities to guide us?
**Irena** My dear, I worry about you. Throwing yourself at anyone who takes your fancy. Gennaro, Jestin, Steve, now Heidi. As though you daren't spend a moment alone.
**Peggy** Steve's not some overgrown boy with eyes bigger than his tummy. Nor some brainless muscle-man. This isn't a sordid sex episode. He and I have the most marvellous discussions. I can't believe you'd be so wide of the mark. I thought you were more far-seeing. I've never been so happy in my life. Surely Gennaro won't send him away, just to spite me? Because *he* wasn't man enough to enjoy a relationship with a mature woman? He can't be *that* puerile. I'm going to have it out with him.
**Irena** I shouldn't. I should wait and see.

*Peggy considers then nods. They embrace*

*Irena goes*

*Heidi returns from the washroom*

*There is a sound from the street*

**Heidi** (*looking out, opening the window; calling*) Non toccate! Via! Andate via! (*She turns back and makes for the door*) Those shits. Tinkering with mein phut-phut.
**Peggy** Heidi .. when you come to my place tonight, will you give Steve a lift? I mean, make sure he comes. I'll have supper ready for us all.
**Heidi** Hey, listen, I shan't be — you know, strawberry?
**Peggy** What?
**Heidi** De trop?
**Peggy** Gooseberry? God, I've just been telling Irena, he's not a bottom-pinching Italian oik. He doesn't see a woman and think Bed with a big B. We'll all have some meravigliose discussioni. Over una bottiglia di Chianti. Ja? Va bene. (*She kisses Heidi*)

*Heidi is surprised but responds, then goes*

*Peggy sings "Che Sera Sera", performs a pirouette and bumps into a table, hurting her leg and knocking her glasses on to the floor. She goes down to search for them*

SCENE 18

*A classroom*

*Steve sits behind a table, giving a private lesson. He skims the pages of "A Room With A View" and considers it. He sings the first line of Noël Coward's "A Room With A View" in a Noël Coward manner*

**Steve** (*speaking*) Same title. Which came first, song or novel? Anyway, I'm glad you read it, Professore, and have to agree with you. Second time round it's not a masterpiece, more a period piece. Not much to do with life today in England. Too — shy. Nervous. Sensitive. An old-fashioned idea of the Englishman as one who shivered on the brink, afraid to get his feet wet. No balls ... coglioni, sì ... the kind of jolly decent chap who let Fascism happen by being meticulous ... um, scrupulosa? Snobbish? ... Wouldn't notice Hitler because he wasn't a gent. What happened here after Forster wasn't personal relationships or Pan prancing through the fields. It was Il Duce, am I right? I Fascisti? ... scusi. Un po' più lentamente, sì. It's — what shall I say? — omosessuale? I'm very fond of them as a class. Some of my best friends ... sì, qualcuno dei migliori amici, know what I mean? ... Knew a lot of them in the army, out in Singapore. You mustn't see all English as perverts. One told me in a bar the other day: the typical Inglese is the man who kills women and fucks them afterwards while wearing a bowler hat ... a bombetta, sì. And fottere, sì. The tyrants of India, friends of Tito, eaters of bad food! And that's a period piece too. Like this book. Full of nice ideas, about a way of life based on trade, which these ladies and gents could pretend not to see while living on the profits. But now our empire's gone and most of us say good-riddance so we needn't ever again have to fight to keep it. We feel no loyalty to any of that ... It's our turn now. And, like Lenin said, we don't want a slice of the cake. We want the bakery.

*Black-out*

SCENE 19

*The staff rest room*

*Night lighting on the room. The window is open. Street sounds*

*Steve turns into it with the book*

*Gennaro peers about the room, then comes in*

**Gennaro** Steven —
**Steve** I'm about to go. Waiting to get a lift from Fräulein Schumann on her phut-phut.
**Gennaro** Ah, yes? She's still here?
**Steve** (*pointing to the other door*) Gabinetto. Having pee-pee. Just finished a late class.
**Gennaro** Between you and me, she may not stay here long.
**Steve** I thought it was me you were posting?
**Gennaro** Eh beh! I can do only what Milan tells me. Otherwise she would have been dismissed already.

*Steve starts to ask why*

You say she's taking you to Peggy's place?
**Steve** Yes. She's moving in there for a while.
**Gennaro** Peggy is your girlfriend?
**Steve** Friend, yes. Girl, no. She fed me and lent me money for a few days. She wouldn't let me pay —
**Gennaro** May I tip the wink? Show you the red light? When she first came, she helped my English. Once or twice I went to the room I found her and we drank some vino rosso. She assumed I mean to leave my wife for her. Made a song and dance. You say, "Flew off the handle"?
**Steve** She's a bit of a headless chicken, yes.
**Gennaro** A headless — ?
**Steve** But she and I — no ...
**Gennaro** (*nodding and looking at the book*) This is the novel then? About Firenze? I must read it.
**Steve** Yes, you should. It's no masterpiece, more a period piece —

*Heidi enters from the washroom*

**Gennaro** I must lock up. Buona notte.

*Gennaro goes*

*Heidi checks through a duffle-bag. Steve watches. Heidi proceeds to sit on a table and plait her hair*

**Heidi** What's eating him? Christ, he was so nice ... and suddenly he doesn't talk no more.
**Steve** He talks to *me*. What did you say to him?

**Heidi**  We discuss politics. A big mistake I think. Maybe I try to be too clever. I've been living such a crazy kind of life in London I had no time to study. But that's all over. I'm going to start again my piano. And you can take that snooty English look off your face. You'll laugh at the other side when I'm playing at Albert Hall. Rachmaninoff, ja? Scarlatti? Hey, d'you like Nat King Cole? From now on I must work. It's work makes you free, not crazy sleeping around.

**Steve**  Arbeit macht frei.

**Heidi**  Ja. Naturlich. But I was only a mixed-up kid from Germany who didn't know no better. You have no idea how strict mein Papa could be. Using the cane and so. If he saw what I did after I left home, he'd have beat me till I cried. But in a way it was his fault. I had to be free of him. And in London look after these horrible old Cockney women in hospital, cleaning up their ca-ca and so. And every hour off duty I wanted only to spend in bed. And I don't mean like you're thinking. I mean fatiguée, stanca morta.

**Steve**  (*keeping his distance*) Was he a Nazi? Dein Papa?

**Heidi**  Only in the early days. Until he saw the way they were going.

**Steve**  Losing?

**Heidi**  Hey, listen, everyone was Nazi at the start. If you'd been born when and where I was, you'd have been in the Hitlerjugend, like me.

**Steve**  You *were*?

**Heidi**  Bestimmt.

**Steve**  (*amused*) Killing! So tell us, what was it like?

**Heidi**  Like? Like your girl scouts. Little Brown Ones?

**Steve**  Brownies.

**Heidi**  They were for the British Empire, we were for the German one, that's all. I enjoyed myself. And the boys were so pretty in their shirts.

**Steve**  Not in the films they weren't. The Riefenstahl films. They looked doolally. Raving. Beating drums, with their eyes on stalks. And the shirts came out all grey.

**Heidi**  Hey listen, I was only a child. Thirteen when the war ended. I had a certificate signed by The Fuhrer at a Jugend rally he came to in person.

**Steve**  Wow! Have you still got it?

**Heidi**  Are you crazy, Liebling? When the Americans came, we buried it in a field. With some other stuff like swastika flags and so. Papa said, in case things changed and they went away, it would be there to dig up again. Nobody could know the future then.

*Steve laughs. Heidi laughs too, without knowing why*

**Steve**  Was this what you talked about with Gennaro?

**Heidi**  Nein. About you English. I told him I thought you had sold out to American Jews.

*Steve laughs*

Ha ha. Very funny. You English laugh all the time. What kind of an answer is that when your country's lost everything / you ever had?
**Steve**  Don't you know Gennaro's a Jew?

*Heidi pauses and considers*

**Heidi**  Ma — è Italiano!
**Steve**  The Italians have Jews. *We* have Jews. America. China. Everyone has Jews ...
**Heidi**  It's true. They're everywhere.
**Steve**  Except Germany.
**Heidi**  Der Fuhrer's plan for them was enlightened, you say that? Illuminato? A new home in Madagascar. Listen, I'm not against Jews.

*Steve laughs*

Ha ha. Laugh again.
**Steve**  After you've just been talking like the Protocols of the Elders of Zion.
**Heidi**  How, when I don't even know what that is? How stupid!
**Steve**  Documents proving the Jews were behind everything bad through money-lending.
**Heidi**  So! There you are then.
**Steve**  But they were fakes. Ersatz. The Russians had made them up to justify the pogroms but that didn't stop your stupid Nazis trotting them out all those years later. (*He laughs again*)

*Heidi is silent, looking in a hand-glass at her braids, which make her like a figure from a fairy-tale*

**Heidi**  The Jews got up to some monkey business too, I think. This Diary of Anna Frank. The little Dutch girl? Didn't you know this was an American-Jewish forgery? And all that business with the camps ... Now you're looking at me in that snooty English way as if to say she's only a silly baby, she knows nothing. Hey, listen, don't laugh at Heidi. I try to be clever but it's this crazy life I was living. Please, caro ... You make me feel so small. You're so superior, so determined. You know so much. You'll take me in hand, won't you, and put an end to that crazy sleeping around and so. Bitte bitte, Liebling ... (*She makes love to him*)

*Steve doesn't respond*

Don't let me turn back to that simple girl from Munich who didn't even know how to stop babies coming. Hey, venga. Andiamo. Peggy's got supper waiting. Pasta with meatballs. Gelato. Chianti. She's really nice, I think. Not beautiful but joli-laide. You know, pretty-ugly?

**Steve** Pretty ugly is about right, yes. Sadly.

**Heidi** That's not very nice to say.

**Steve** No. And I wish I hadn't.

**Heidi** (*tossing him the key of her Vespa*) D'you think you can handle mein phut-phut?

*Steve shakes his head and tosses the key back*

So you will take the back seat. You don't mind? Don't mind if a woman drives? It doesn't hurt your manhood, having a woman take control? (*She laughs as though she's scored a point and packs her bag*) You know you must lean when I do and hold tight with your knees.

*Steve comes to Heidi from behind. She gives instructions; he acts them out*

*The Lights change. A Bach chorale begins*

*Peggy brings on a gingham tablecloth, cutlery, a Chianti-bottle lamp, etc, and starts laying the table*

*Heidi breaks away and goes to the door. Steve follows and turns out the lights in the room. He thrusts her back across a table, seizes her hands and pushes them back above her head. He stands looking down on her. She laughs and embraces him with her legs*

*Peggy looks at the knife and breathes on it, polishes it with her sleeve and lays it in place*

**Peggy** Is this a knife? Yes. This is a knife.

*The chorale continues*

END OF ACT I

# ACT II

*A classroom*

*Steve takes a lesson, leading his class of Italians in community singing.*
*We hear them trying to follow, then dropping out*

**Steve**  Oh I do like to be beside the seaside,
I do like to be beside the sea.
I do like to walk along the prom-prom-prom
Where the brass band plays tiddley-om-pom-pom
I do like to be beside the seaside ... (*Etc.*)

*By now he's singing alone. At the end the students applaud*

Bravo! Ancora! (*He listens to a question*) Cosa vuol dire? Fa niente.
The meaning does not matter. Non è importante. È per la pratica.
Adesso — vediamo un po' — proviamo invece page thirteen in the
pages I gave you. Tredici. Got it? Pronto? Allora — uno — due
— tre!
Wotcher, all the neighbours cried
Who you gonna meet, Bill ?
Have you bought the street, Bill ?
Laugh? I thought I should have died.
Knocked 'em in the Old Kent Road.

*Black-out*

## Scene 2

*A classroom*

*The Lights come up on Madge holding a potted plant with no flowers*

**Madge**  What. Is this? Animal, vegetable or mineral? ... I won't ask
Giulietta Montana, too busy with her mouth open catching flies to
profit from the lesson her poor parents have coughed up for. OK, this

is the same potted plant that each of you has on your desk. Except,
of course, for Anna-Magdalena Filiberto who forgot to bring hers in.
Notice: no flowers. And no blooms on any of our plants. Why, Mario
Dante? ... "Perché"? What's "perché"? ... Because, yes! Because this
is now the season of — what, Mario? ... The fall? What fall is that? The
Fall of Man? "Falling in love with love is falling for make-believe"?
We are here to learn English, not American. The word is — sì, Alfredo?
... well, close. Except we say aw-tum, not ah-oo-tom. We began today
with the thought that Florence means City of Flowers. Though I must
say there are far more in my own Melbourne. London. Even Cairo.
Italian parks seem to be mostly gravel and statues of writhing torsos.
Nothing like the carpet of bluebells and snowdrops of an English
meadow. (*Reciting*)
> For oft, when on my couch I lie
> In vacant or in pensive mood
> They flash upon that inner eye —

### SCENE 3

*The staff rest room. Afternoon*

*The Lights come up on Madge, Steve, Peggy, Irena, Heidi and Jestin.
Steve is imitating Madge for the amusement of the others. For a line they
recite together, then Madge exits*

**Steve**                    That is the bliss of solitude
                             And then my heart with pleasure feawls
                             And dances with the daffodeawls.

*Peggy, Irena and Heidi laugh*

**Peggy**  Killing. You're a wonderful mimic. Quite wasted as a teacher.

*The bell rings*

*All but Steve prepare to go to class*

**Steve**  I shan't always be, trust me.
**Peggy**  Famous last words. Few escape. Look at Madge!
**Steve**  James Joyce and Wilfred Owen also taught in language schools.
   But not forever. Joyce was writing *Ulysses* in Trieste and Owen was
   in Bordeaux.

**Jestin** So what will you do instead?
**Heidi** He returns to London and opens a coffee bar.
**Steve** I wish! First man does will be a millionaire. Trouble is, I can
    barely afford a cappuccino leave alone a Gaggia machine. All I own is
    a secondhand Olivetti. So I'll probably just have to settle for being a
    writer, not a businessman.
**Peggy** We must find you a wealthy widow. A sugar mummy.

*Steve sits at the desk*

*Peggy kisses the top of his head as he sits*

    Have you got a lesson now?
**Steve** Not till three.
**Peggy** So — tavola calda till tonight? How about you, Heidi?
**Heidi** No, grazie.
**Steve** Oh, come on. Not even for a sandwich? (*He puts out his tongue
    and makes a gesture of oral sex at Heidi*)

*Heidi laughs*

**Peggy** (*unseeing*) What's funny? I suppose it is a rather droll word.
    The Earl of Sandwich invented it so he could eat without leaving the
    gaming-table.
**Heidi** I can't even rent another room till I know Gennaro lets me stay
    as teacher.
**Peggy** What about you, Jestin?
**Jestin** Thank you, my dear, I have an excursion I want / to make.
**Peggy** Allora — I'll find you here, Steve.
**Steve** In an hour.
**Peggy** Arrivederla, caro. (*She blows him a kiss*)

*Peggy goes*

**Heidi** Not a single lesson he allows me. Please say a word for me,
    Liebling? If you want me to stay?
**Steve** OK.
**Heidi** Now I go to look at rooms to let. It isn't right to stay with Peggy
    no longer.

*Heidi goes*

**Irena** I'm relieved she has at least that much sense of right and wrong.
    And better late than never.

**Jestin** Perhaps we shouldn't expect it. Her generation of Germans were
taught a dubious moral code.

**Irena** Wasn't her father a theologian?

**Jestin** What could be more morally dubious than a belief in God, in
magic? To a humanist, religion means pain and punishment. Art's a
better teacher by far.

**Irena** The Nazis sobbed when Jewish musicians played Schubert in
Auschwitz. Art's no more reliable than God.

*Irena goes*

**Jestin** I don't believe that. I don't believe Irena does either. I'm going
to eat a slice of pizza in the cloisters of Santissima Annunziata. And
in the Hospital of the Innocents beside it there are Ghirlandaios
and Botticellis and Della Robbia's medallions of the swathed and
abandoned children. A lovely place. Soothing to the spirit. Why don't
you join me?

**Steve** I better wait for Peggy.

**Jestin** For another free lunch? (*He goes to the window; after a pause*)
Steven ... d'you know what I mean by "grace"?

**Steve** What people used to say before meals?

**Jestin** In the broader sense, beauty of form or behaviour. A good thing
to have and practise. One feels it in these works we've been looking at.
The artists may have been flawed characters, like us all, but were made
better by a lifetime lived with saints and holy children ... depicting a
state of innocence. Often unbelievers working for money, they were
paid to carve angels and in the process acquired grace.

**Steve** You saying I can too by looking at their pictures?

**Jestin** I think everyone may. Why else do so many come / from so far
away ...?

**Steve** It's on their curriculum? Or because they'll go anywhere to see
something old and handmade?

**Jestin** Or because grace is there.

**Steve** I was a courier once in London. Got sick to death of the tourists'
disappointed faces as they climbed from the coach by Westminster
Abbey. This vast place they'd seen on newsreels. So small! "Una
chiesa parrocchiale!" (*Explaining*) A parish church. So instead I used
to take them to Saint Pancras Station and say it was the Abbey. Much
bigger, Victorian Gothic, plenty of red brick. "Bella, bellissima!"

**Jestin** Well, if it raised their spirits.

**Steve** That's what I thought, yeah.

**Jestin** Then be like them. Let these works of art change you, dear boy.
Stop hurting Peggy.

**Steve** Hurt? She seems to be on Cloud Nine. I've never encouraged her. She wants discussions. Discussions is what we have. And food and wine, yes. Fair exchange.

**Jestin** And what about Heidi?

**Steve** We also give each other what we want.

**Jestin** And when Peggy finds out?

**Steve** Non è il mio problema.

**Jestin** That sort of talk stunts your growth, Steven. Your moral growth. Dear boy, you have the wherewithal to be a good man. A mature man, with all that implies. An adult, not a greedy child. Don't choose the uncharitable way. You can make others laugh, which may be either a joyful sound or an angry snarl that hurts and destroys.

**Steve** Or could be laughter releases the rage we're too kind to show them openly.

**Jestin** What are you raging *about*? When you've been given so much? Because someone behaves in a way you find absurd? Dear boy, I fear for you.

**Steve** Don't trouble yourself. Really. I'm fine.

**Jestin** You must believe in something.

**Steve** Or else live *without* beliefs and loyalties. Now we've got The Bomb, being loyal to one side or other may finish us off with one big bang, not just a few million at a time. And it was being faithful to all that Nordic bullshit made Nazis possible in the first place. Or Mussolini telling modern Italians they were Ancient Romans — all loyalty. Heavy baggage. Who needs it? Anyway that war was kids' stuff beside what's coming.

*Steve goes to the washroom*

*Jestin stands alone and shakes his head*

SCENE 4

*A classroom*

*Spotlight on Heidi teaching with a fork, spoon and knife*

**Heidi** Was ist das? Das ist eine Gabel. Ist es ein Löffel? Nein, es ist nicht ein Löffel. Das ist eine Gabel.

*Gennaro enters the light*

**Gennaro** Gestatten sie, bitte, Fräulein.
**Heidi** Sì, Signor Manetti? Cosa vuole?
**Gennaro** I wanted a word with you. You said you had to know if you
were to be returned to Milan? Dunque ... Milano says there are more
students who want to take German here than there, so you will stay.
Per il momento.
**Heidi** Oh, fantastiche. Sehr gut. Even though you tried hard to get rid
of me? I think so, ja?
**Gennaro** (*anxious in case the class understands*) I leave you now to
your lesson.
**Heidi** Why d'you do that, Liebling? I never meant nothing by what I
said about Hitler. / I was only a baby when he ——
**Gennaro** Danke schön, Fräulein.

*Gennaro goes*

*After a pause Heidi turns to the front again*

**Heidi** Ist es ein Messer? Nein, das ist eine Gabel.

SCENE 5

*A classroom*

*Spotlight on Steve, singing and conducting his class. They try to follow
(and we hear them)*

**Steve**              It's the same the whole world over,
                       It's the poor what gets the blame.
                       It's the rich what gets the pleasure.
                       Ain't it all a bleeding shame.

(*Applauding the students' efforts*) Bravissimo! Bene fatto.

SCENE 6

*Staff rest room*

*Daylight on Peggy coming from the washroom. Heidi stands at the
window shouting down*

**Heidi** Ti ho visto! Levati dalle palle! Chiamo la polizia, capito? (*She turns back into the room*) Always mein phut-phut. Why can't they leave it alone?

**Peggy** It was so funny last night, you and Steve going off on it, him holding a piece of your luggage in each hand, like a pack-mule with wheels. I thought you'd surely come to grief.

**Heidi** Last night I drive him nice and slow.

**Peggy** I was amazed to see him back in one piece. Just you dare let him come to any harm and —— (*She raises one of the knives from the table, as if to stab Heidi, then drops it and laughs*)

*Heidi, startled at first, laughs too. Peggy carves initials on the table top*

**Heidi** How was it after I left?

**Peggy** Oh, he couldn't stay long. He'd promised Irena he'd help entertain some white Russian emigrés, some old count still clinging to his title after forty years of Communism. So we had some very stimulating conversation, then he went to Via Belvedere.

*Heidi looks at the timetable and fetches a text book*

I'm sorry I couldn't let you bed down longer at my place.

**Heidi** God, no, you don't want a lodger hanging round, coming in at all hours. You like to be alone, ja?

**Peggy** What makes you think that? Because I so often am? I loved having you there. It's just that Steven was embarrassed. You know, two's company? It's the way some Englishmen are with their girlfriends. You could have stayed but when you found another room so easily ...

**Heidi** Fa niente, davvero, now that Gennaro's got to keep me here in Florence.

**Peggy** And you thought he wanted to get rid of you!

**Heidi** He didn't have no choice. They tell him from Milan.

**Peggy** So he says, to save his bella figura. He often makes a pass at girls but never bears a grudge when we turn him down. Italian men ... just boys. They want Madonnas at home and Magdalenes everywhere else.

*Street organ and traffic sounds. Heidi looks from the window, then turns and seems about to go*

Did you have that word of warning with him?

**Heidi** Gennaro?

**Peggy** Steve. About the student girls? He still leers at them in the most obvious and childish manner. It means nothing, I know that, but he's going on the right way to get a knife in his back / from some jealous lover ——
**Heidi** Sure, I tell him if I see him / some time.
**Peggy** Make it seem to come from you.
**Heidi** Why should I be telling him that?
**Peggy** Concern for his safety. As a friend.

*Heidi shrugs and makes to leave again*

You'll be all right in that room, won't you? If I were you, I'd feel lost all alone in that enormous bed.

*Heidi nods her head and goes*

*Peggy blows away sawdust and looks at her carving*

SCENE 7

*A classroom*

*Spotlight on Steve leading a series of questions and answers, conducting the responses from a class of Italians*

**Steve** So — who'll carry the banner?
**Class** Sister Anna will carry the banner.
**Steve** (*falsetto*) I carried it last week.
**Class** You'll carry it every week.
**Steve** (*falsetto*) But I'm in the family way.
**Class** You're in every fucker's way.
**Steve** (*falsetto*) Please! I'm only thirteen.
**Class** This is no time for superstition.
**Steve** (*falsetto*) I'll tell the vicar.
**Class** I *am* the vicar.
**Steve** (*in his own voice*) Molto bene! Benissimo! Congratulazioni!

*The bell rings*

SCENE 8

*Staff rest room*

*Steve turns back into the staff room to listen to Gennaro*

**Gennaro** But you must be careful how far you go. Some of the other teachers are complaining you distract their classes singing and shouting.
**Steve** Not shouting. Chanting. Chorus speaking. Like the strophe and antistrophe in Greek drama.
**Gennaro** And the songs?
**Steve** Rugby songs.
**Gennaro** (*impressed*) From Rugby, the English private school?
**Steve** Right. I'm using rhythm and rhyme and melody as an aid to fluent speech.
**Gennaro** I only say: be careful. While some voices sing and shout very loud, others may not speak at all and will not be heard and will fall behind.
**Steve** Don't worry, I'll hear them. Not that I think that kind of phoney equality is the way to Utopia ... holding back the quick to make the slow and stupid feel faster. The quick ones go mad and the others can tell they're being patronized. They aren't *that* stupid.
**Gennaro** Thank you for the lesson. I am not one of them.
**Steve** No, sorry. Scusami.
**Gennaro** And for the money they pay they don't expect the Promised Land. You say that?
**Steve** We *could*.
**Gennaro** This is not an Oxford college. Or Rugby School. Just a language shop.
**Steve** My lessons are at least amusing.
**Gennaro** It's not a cabaret either.

*Madge enters from a classroom*

**Madge** Jesus, Gennaro! You've got me teaching a lingo I don't even savvy, leave alone speak. What'll happen when the poor buggers try to book a room in Barcelona? I'd sooner try Japanese. At least I've taught in Yokohama.
**Gennaro** There's not enough student demand to justify a Spanish teacher. The less they know in Milan the better. We none of us want no trouble, OK?

*Irena comes in*

**Steve**  We've been discussing the ideal of equality through education.
**Madge**  God save us from that.

*Madge goes to the washroom*

**Steve**  Starts with Rousseau, Proudhon.
**Gennaro**  Tolstoy, Marx ...
**Irena**  But always ends with Stalin.
**Gennaro**  Man being what he is, yes, I think so.
**Steve**  You all see it in terms of these great European abstracts. We
English think more in jokes. Stories. Per esempio ... Once upon a
time — at secondary school — we had a knock-out tournament of
five-a-side football teams from various schools. I was good at games
so was in the best team, top of the league table. The bottom one was
from a special school, made up entirely of the handicapped. Or, if
you prefer, "encountering difficulties". A mongol, a spastic, a diabetic
amputee in a wheelchair — and their captain was partially-sighted. It
was understood that no one would run up a heavy score against *them*.
Beat them, yes, they'd expect that, any other result would be insulting,
but only by a reasonable margin, two or three goals, which we all
somehow managed to do in our friendly matches with them.

*Jestin comes in and listens, replacing text books in the bookcase*

Next-to-bottom was an able-bodied team who couldn't play for toffee.
Well, imagine our horror and revulsion when this lot beat the cripples
thirty-two nil. And this wasn't rugby. Not points. I'm talking goals!
We ostracized the buggers, gave them a real hard time, but there was
no disputing the fact they'd won the tournament on aggregate. After
the dust had settled, the captain told me that first off his team had all
been as shocked as we were by his passion to win, but come the dawn
they all realized winning meant more to them than some charade of
meritocracy. And, after all, he said, it was only a matter of degree, his
team were handicapped too, by being so bad at games. So tough shit,
they were the champions! (*He does a supporters' roar, fists held up*)

*Gennaro shakes his head and goes*

**Irena**  Talk of Communism makes Gennaro uneasy. He feels he should
have done more against the Fascisti.
**Jestin**  He never joined them surely?

**Irena**  No, nor the partisans. He saw out the war by lying low.
**Jestin**  In fact avoiding battle is an honourable Italian tradition. Mercenary factions in the Renaissance always agreed not to encounter each other and go safe home.
**Steve**  Nothing's pure black or white, is it? Even Mussolini had his points. He'd nearly wiped out the Mafia. But when the Allies invaded Sicily, the gangster Lucky Luciano did a deal, was released from jail and fixed up an instant surrender to the Yanks. So you could say the Allies saved Cosa Nostra for democracy. Who did most harm, Il Duce or the Allies? And the Duce finished strung up from a lamp post. And the Mafia's stronger now than Fascism ever was. (*He smiles*)

*Peggy and Heidi come in through the main door*

**Jestin**  Why do you revel in every setback for decency? Where's your loving kindness? You won't build a new world on hatred.
**Steve**  Nor on lies either.
**Jestin**  There can be good lies. The fact an idea's upsetting and venomous doesn't make it true.
**Peggy**  Jestin, you really show your age when you talk to Steve like that. People of our generation don't need rose-tinted glasses. We look at life head-on and the truth / isn't always pleasant.
**Steve**  Leave it, Peg.

*The bell rings to start a new period*

*Steve goes to his class*

**Heidi**  Pee-pee-pee. And I only just arrive. So they must wait. Devo andare al gabinetto, capeesh?

*Heidi goes to the washroom*

*Madge returns*

**Madge**  At least my next lot's in English. Any more of that dago stuff and I'm downing tools, I don't care how much it drops Gennaro in the big jobs.
**Jestin**  Irena, at five o'clock let's you and I spend some time in San Marco, top up our spirits, take away the bad taste.
**Irena**  Why not Santa Maria del Carmine? The Masaccio frescoes.
**Jestin**  They the ones that extol that dreadful old killjoy St Paul? I'll take some convincing.

*Jestin shakes his head and goes*

*Irena and Peggy are left alone*

**Peggy**  He wasn't too late then?
**Irena**  Who?
**Peggy**  Steve.
**Irena**  Too late?
**Peggy**  Last night? To help you with your Russian guests? What time did he arrive? He left me about ten. So he'd have been with you at — what — half-past? So was he on time?
**Irena**  My dear ...

*Peggy waits, then starts crying*

*Heidi comes from the washroom*

*Peggy controls herself*

**Heidi**  Ca-ca-ca! Merda! Allora — meglio tardi che mai.

*She grabs her text and exercise books and goes to class*

**Irena**  I wish you wouldn't upset yourself. He isn't worth it.
**Peggy**  I love him. How d'you think he feels about me?
**Irena**  I couldn't say. He doesn't talk to me about those things. Art, politics / or history yes —
**Peggy**  Just like with me. Discussions. Irena, will you do me a kindness?
**Irena**  I won't spy on him.
**Peggy**  No, no. Just ask him. Ask him what his feelings are. I believe he may be shy. Perhaps I frightened him. If you told him how I feel, it might loosen his tongue. Put the question as though you'd been observing us both, an interested onlooker. An older woman. Don't let on it came from me. Would you do that for me?

*Irena takes and kisses her hand*

Scene 9

*A classroom*

*Spotlight on Madge, teaching a private pupil*

**Madge** Yes, Signora Bertorelli, I'm not a total ignoramus. I know Italian women consider anyone of their sex who's childless to be a total write-off. But not every woman wants to be plagued by a swarm of little monsters. Sticky fingers into everything. A pervasive aroma of ca-ca. Never a moment's peace. That's a male conspiracy. Aided and abetted by your Pope. Papa, don't you call him? Every man a papa, every woman a mamma. A confidence trick to keep women down. So your pity's wasted on me. In my eyes it's you who's to be pitied. Not Yours Truly.

*Black-out*

Scene 10

*A classroom*

*A spotlight comes up on Steve, leading his class in song*

**Steve** All together now ——
**All**           That was a cute little rhyme.
               Sing us another one, do!

**Steve**        When Titian was mixing rosemadder
               His model posed nude on a ladder.
               The position to Titian
               Suggested coition
               So he nipped up the ladder and had'er.

**All**          That was a cute little rhyme.
               Sing us another one, do.
**Steve** Francesco — you try.

*Black-out*

SCENE 11

*A classroom*

*Spotlight on Jestin, seated, reading to a student*

**Jestin**          Child of the pure unclouded brow
                    And dreaming eyes of wonder!
                    Though time be fleet and I and thou
                    Are half a life asunder,
                    Thy loving smile will surely hail
                    The love-gift of a fairy-tale.

*He looks up at the student, eyes tearful*

          You do understand, my dear? Or is it too difficult? Too advanced?

*The light fades almost to darkness. Silence*

SCENE 12

*The staff rest room*

*There is lamplight through the window on the tower and cathedral dome against a night sky. We hear male and female sounds of fucking from the door to the washroom*

*Irena opens the other door, comes in, turns on the light and makes for the washroom door. She is about to open it, then hears the excited sounds. She recoils, at once turns off the light and retreats, closing the door. Darkness*

SCENE 13

*A classroom*

*Light on Jestin, as before*

**Jestin**          Come hearken then, ere voice of dread,
                    With bitter tidings laden,
                    Shall summon to unwelcome bed

> A melancholy maiden.
> We are but older children, dear,
> Who fret to find our bedtime near.

SCENE 14

*The staff rest room*

*Daylight on Irena and Peggy, who's scanning a book but covertly listening*

*Music of the street organ*

**Irena** He's very fond of you. He thinks of you as one of his closest friends. Without your help, he said, he could not have stayed in Florence. Not on what he earns from Lingua Franca.

*Peggy turns to her and waits*

He said you are one of the people here he will remember most when he leaves. As a true companion. He values his freedom too highly ... to have, you know what I mean, relazione ... serious affaires? You will forgive my speaking frankly, you are well rid of him. Non è simpatico. You are worth ten of him.

**Peggy** How long did you talk to him?

**Irena** As I said, a mere few minutes —

**Peggy** And that's long enough to learn all this about him?

**Irena** I'd already formed certain opinions of Signor Flowers / during the time —

**Peggy** Opinions? Not prejudices then? Not bigotry? You wouldn't by any chance have already formed a view of him that means you can't make sense of anything he says?

**Irena** What he says is pretty clear.

**Peggy** How in hell would you know? How would you understand shades of meaning? You speak very good English, Irena, but, let's face it, you're not, are you? English? You're a Russian thinking in Italian.

**Irena** You asked me to / speak to him so I did —

**Peggy** I didn't ask for a slanderous attack on his character. You people think ...

**Irena** "You people"?

**Peggy** ... Because we English aren't blubbing and beating our breasts all day we're frigid.

**Irena** What "people"?

**Peggy** All of you.
**Irena** Jews?
**Peggy** God! You must be paranoid. No. Foreigners! You think if a man
and woman don't jump into bed the first time they meet, they're dead/
from the neck down.
**Irena** I'm sorry. Don't blame the messenger for the message. I was
trying to be kind.
**Peggy** No one asked you to be kind. Steve and I don't find it easy to
open our hearts to each other, but the course of true love isn't helped
by everyone jumping to the wrong conclusions. I'd have expected
a woman of your age to have more sense. It's not as though you're
simple-minded like Jestin ... or an overgrown child like Gennaro ... or
feckless Heidi who sees no further / than the masks we wear to hide
our true feelings ——
**Irena** (*losing her patience*) Stop this at once, you stupid girl. Since you
mention her, why don't you ask him if he can describe in detail the
large oil painting of The Rape of the Sabine Women over her bed?
Or ask her landlady who is an acquaintance of mine about the animal
sounds from her room that disturb her Canasta games? So I didn't need
to speak to him on your behalf. And I was trying to break it gently.

*Peggy is at last silenced. Irena looks at her watch*

Jestin and I were going to see Fra Angelico's frescoes in the monastery
of San Marco. Has he forgotten, d'you think, and gone alone? I wonder
some times if Jestin's reason for going to the university quarter isn't to
watch the students waiting in the Piazza for their lectures ...

*Gennaro's and other Italian voices are raised in argument offstage*

What on earth's going on? (*She opens the main door*)

*Unseen by Irena, Peggy takes up the breadknife from among the stock
of cutlery and goes off to the washroom*

*Heidi comes in through the main door*

**Heidi** Hey, listen, you won't never believe this.
**Irena** What is it? Who are those people?
**Heidi** An Italian family of a student. They come protesting against a
professore.
**Irena** You always said he'd be getting in trouble some day, the way he
talked to the girl students, didn't you, Peggy? (*She looks round and
finds Peggy gone*)

**Heidi** Who?
**Irena** Steven, of course. Isn't that who you mean?
**Heidi** Steve? Nein. Pas du tout.

*Jestin is hustled in by Steve and Madge. Madge shuts the door and turns the key. Jestin's shirt is torn and stained from a bleeding nose*

They accuse Jestin of making a pass on their sister.
**Madge** The bastards have brought in the fucking polizia. They're pressing charges.
**Irena** Whatever happened, Jestin?
**Jestin** As far as I can make out, it was the girl I have for private lessons/ three times a week —
**Madge** Signorina Celino?
**Jestin** Lovely child.
**Steve** Don't keep saying that. When the police ask questions, don't say she's a lovely child.
**Jestin** But she is. I read her some verses — from *Alice Through the Looking-Glass*. You know ... "Child of the pure unclouded brow — "
**Irena** Is that all?
**Steve** Remind me. What are they about?
**Jestin** Age and youth. The sadness of age, the beauty of youth and childhood, the shadow of death. Not even a view I share except as a poetic fancy. I've enjoyed *every* age of my life ... Too silly.
**Heidi** Hey, listen, this will make such scandal.
**Steve** But they can't believe it of Jestin at his age.
**Madge** You want to put money on that?
**Irena** Let's get him into the washroom, clean his face.
**Madge** Wasn't Lewis Carroll a Jessie? Funny for little girls?

*The voices offstage swell and approach. The door is shaken*

*Madge, Irena, Steve and Heidi begin to walk Jestin towards the washroom door*

*Peggy emerges from the washroom with the knife, bloodstained dress, wrists cut. She goes for Heidi*

*Heidi turns away to evade the blade but it sinks into her face. She falls. Steve tries to disarm Peggy but she stabs him in the arm. Gennaro hammers on the door*

\*

*A climactic burst of Verdi. A dazzling light is directed at the audience*

*Gennaro comes with calming gestures, as though facing hostile paparazzi*

**Gennaro** Per favore ... no need for scandal. Signori, these people are not famous. Non sono importante. Your readers will not want to hear this. Allow us to continue our educational work.

*Gennaro goes*

*The dazzling light goes off as he exits*

SCENE 15

*A classroom*

*Madge comes into the downstage lights to address her class*

**Madge** Hands up anyone knows Istanbul ... no one? Me neither. In fact, it will be — for me — virgin territory. Apparently there are Turks of all ages and persuasions who, for reasons best known to themselves, can't wait to garble the tongue that Shakespeare spake. And, I dare say, even more of them champing at the bit to emulate the tongue of your friend Elvis. The one he sticks out and wiggles about. I'm due for a change anyway. My lady companion and I always welcome fresh fields, different cultures. Needless to say, we'd rather not have had the school wound up in quite so operatic a style. I hope some of you at least will continue taking lessons from Signor Manetti. You'd do well with him, not only for yourselves but for kindness' sake as he needs to build a circle of private students. He has a wife and children and as of now no job. And I'd like to observe in passing that it's not Mr Overton who should be leaving under a cloud but that member of the student body who reckoned he touched her up. Course, there was nothing in it. But it's a bloody sight easier throwing shit than getting it cleaned off. *(She listens to a response)* No, dearie, you weren't *meant* to follow. I just wanted to remind you how far there is to go before you spikka da Inglees. Allora — arrivederci, a tutti. But not if I see you first.

SCENE 16

*The staff rest room*

*Evening light. Madge goes to join Gennaro, Irena, Heidi and Steve posing for a group photograph being taken by the foreman of a team of removal men. They all have mugs or glasses of red wine: Heidi wears a black patch over the injured eye, Steve's arm is in a sling. The other removal men strike the furniture*

*From the window comes the sound of the street organ*

**Steve** Dica "formaggio".
**Irena** No. Sorridi!

*They all smile. A flash-bulb lights them*

**Gennaro** (*making a speech*) Grazie. I will speak English because — well, because we all do. Irena wants you to share this Sassicaia. A gesture that shows a level of forgiveness I find I cannot equal. Because what have you brought here but desolation? The tourists come, spend their money and go ... but you ... because of you the school is closed. My bustarelle (*he mimes passing an envelope to an official*) — what d'you say — ?
**Steve** Backhanders? Sweeteners ?
**Gennaro** Ecco! — Weren't fat enough to keep this scandal under the carpet. You say that, under the carpet?
**Madge** Between these four walls might be better. Specially seein' as there ain't no carpet. Just bloody lino.

*Madge goes*

**Gennaro** I tried to stop those newspaper stories about old Jestin but Italians like to believe that all English are Jack Rippers. They thought he was tarred with the same brush. You can say that?

*The walls now become a screen for back projections of Chicago's skyline and lakeside*

*Steve removes his sling and browses through a handful of postcards. The others come to the front of stage as they speak*

So now I must return to selling salami for my father-in-law. I doubt I shall ever be able to teach again, at least in Italy ... I heard from Irena

you're now Stateside and wonder if by chance you hear sometimes of
a school that needs an Italian professore as my wife and I have always
wanted / to live there ...
**Steve** (*to us at first, then to Gennaro*) I moved on, yes, like always. No
baggage, no loyalties. Remembered I had this uncle in Chicago. Dear
Gennaro, sorry, I'm afraid I've no connections here with teaching.

*Gennaro goes*

Irena, you ask if I have a lady-friend here. One or two, yes, but no, as
yet no plans to marry. Still too young — maybe always will be ...
**Irena** Yes, I'm still stuck in the Arno mud. Teaching American. What
your adopted country has done to the world! Seduced and raped it.
**Steve** There was no need for either. Looks to me like the world rolled
over with open legs.
**Irena** Does anyone ever hear from Peggy?
**Steve** Yes. Pretty often.
**Heidi** Me too. I absolutely didn't know how crazy she was about you.
**Irena** I did. I blame myself. Heidi knew as well but that didn't stop you
two behaving / like animals.

*A back projection of a view of Munich*

**Heidi** God in Heaven, this business has stopped me in my tracks, you
know? And losing half of my sight. I'm turning a new leaf. For the
time being I play piano in a night club in my hometown of Munchen.
The guy who runs it prefers the eyepatch to dark glasses, ja? Says it
adds a touch of decadence for the tourists ... like the twenties, ja?

*A back projection of a view of Perugia. The projection of Munich starts
to fade slowly*

*Peggy enters*

**Peggy** Dear Steve, I'm out of the madhouse now.
**Heidi** The Blue Angel naturlich ... Lenya and Dietrich and Sally Bowles/
this crazy English girl?
**Peggy** It wasn't the Ritz but could have been worse.
**Heidi** Listen, I'm going to study Beethoven and Bach and my namesake
Schumann ... Learning to be a good hausfrau ... / cook schnitzel, /
knackvurst mit rotkohl ...
**Peggy** As far as Lingua Franca's concerned, I'm persona non grata ...
vietato ... / proibita.

**Heidi** I'm happy to say mein Papa here is far nicer than before. Even offered money to get rid of the baby because I knew you'd never admit to being the father / and so.

**Peggy** I've worked up quite a clientele of private students in Perugia, though only one or two are able to keep their hands above the table / for more than five minutes ...

**Heidi** And by the way that wasn't very nice when you asked how I knew you were the father when there were so many possibles. None era gentile, quello ... Anyway I'm so thrilled with little Maximilian. Who'd have thought your silly Heidi would ever feel such mutterliebe? / Nessuno.

**Peggy** Jestin used to say hers was an unfortunate generation. Too young to have chosen the Nazis, just old enough to be seduced.

**Heidi** Hey, listen, d'you know these guys the Modern Jazz Quartet?

**Irena** But Jestin believed the best of everyone.

**Heidi** And Dave Brubeck, he's very cool, I think. Is he by any chance Jewish? / He looks like he may be ...

*The Munich projection fades completely*

*Heidi goes*

**Irena** He could always find good. The only atheist I've ever heard use the word "grace".

**Steve** Yeah. And once his own innocence was questioned, he began to wonder if ...

**Irena** ... If he *had* molested that silly girl, I know. Trouble was, he never learnt any Italian ——

**Peggy** Or any other language, which meant he used the method perfectly ... but also that he missed a lot of nuances. Warning signs ... danger signals ... one might feel like discussing the question: when does "innocent" become "obtuse"? ...

*Peggy goes*

**Irena** I wasn't surprised to hear he went a little — what was your word? — Bananas?

**Steve** Is he still hanging around school playgrounds, I wonder?

*A back projection of pictures of London. First people in 50s fashions then into the 60s. Beatles music plays*

*Jestin enters*

**Jestin** The police were decent enough. They only held me for a few hours. It soon struck them the poor mother who reported me for loitering at the playground was hardly in her right mind.

**Irena** That radiance of spirit depended on believing in human decency. His own purity.

**Jestin** Dear boy, I can't fathom this new London. The young all seem to have so much, with their Gaggia machines and Vespa scooters ... yet their novels and plays are all so angry! Gangs making fun of other gangs. As though they want to show that, in spite of all that's been achieved by the light of reason, there will still always be darkness and evil. If that's the coming world, I'm glad I shan't be in it much longer.

**Irena** D'you remember when I took you both to see the Massacio fresco?

*A back-projection of the Massacio picture now appears, Adam and Eve limping away, hiding their faces in shame. It gets bigger during the next*

**Steve** The Expulsion from the Garden, yes.

**Jestin** Such a wicked story. No wonder we live in fear of mutual extermination.

**Steve** (*to Irena again*) He thought The Fall of Man was a really crap idea. And though in my heart I couldn't disagree, I knew it was time to face facts. To grow up. Join the rest of the fallen world.

**Irena** Well, you have now. You're the thugs of Europe.

*Irena goes*

**Steve** Better than the Babes in the Wood we'd been ever since we stopped being bosses. We had to find a future that included us. I couldn't picture joining Europe. I'd tried the East. The blacks and browns, espressos and cappuccinos didn't fancy us lattes ... and alone we were lost. So what else was there but to become Americanos ... ? (*He goes on browsing through the cards, throwing some away*)

*The Massacio now dominates all the walls*

*Growing out of the melange of music comes the street organ from Scene One, playing "Yankee Doodle"*

*Steve discards all the cards and looks at his own empty hands*

CURTAIN

# FURNITURE AND PROPERTY LIST

## ACT I

### SCENE 1

*On stage*: Door to wash room with frosted-glass panel in one side wall
Window with view of Giotto's bell-tower and the façade of
Brunelleschi's cathedral beyond the upper floors of a street
in Florence
Main door in right wall with doorknob and key in keyhole
Switch (beside the door)
Practical overhead fan
Tables. *On them*: text and exercise books and a copy of
*A Room With A View*
*On one of the tables*: selection of knives, forks and spoons,
bread knife
Upright chairs
Couch
Book case containing books including a *Dictionary
of Quotations*
Timetable
Drab formal group photos of earlier teaching staffs (on the walls)
Travel posters of Italian towns (on the walls)

### SCENE 2

*Off stage*: Large shoulder-bag, cigarettes (**Peggy**)

*Personal*: **Steve**: banknotes, matches (in pocket)
**Peggy**: tinted glasses, sun hat

### SCENE 3

*Personal*: **Irena**: beads and jewellery, headscarf

### SCENE 4

*Set*: Work for marking (for **Peggy**)

SCENE 5

*On stage*:     As before

SCENE 6

*Set*:          Cigarette (for **Steve**)

*Off stage*:    Pocket glass (**Irena**)
                Cigarettes (**Madge**)
                Old school satchel crammed with personal items (**Jestin**)

SCENE 7

*On stage*:     As before

SCENE 8

*On stage*:     As before

SCENE 9

*Set*:          Cigarette (for **Steve**)

SCENE 10

*On stage*:     As before

SCENE 11

*Set*:          Hand mirror, make-up (for **Peggy**)
                Hat with a raccoon's tail hanging behind
                Dark glasses

*Off stage*:    Text books (**Steve**)
                Wet comb (**Steve**)

SCENE 12

*Set*:          Handbag containing make-up and glass

SCENE 13

*Personal*:     **Madge**: watch

SCENE 14

*Set*:          Cigarettes (for **Peggy** and **Irena**)

*Off stage*:    Cigarette (**Steve**)

*Personal*:    **Peggy**: glasses
              **Steve**: dark glasses

SCENE 15

*On stage*:    As before

SCENE 16

*Set*:        Apple
              Banana

SCENE 17

*Set*:        **Peggy**'s glasses (on table)

*Strike*:      Apple
              Banana

*Off stage*:    Book, cutlery (**Steve**)

SCENE 18

*On stage*:    As before

Scene 19

*Set*:        Open window
              Duffle-bag

*Off stage*:    Hand-glass, key to Vespa (**Heidi**)
              Gingham tablecloth, cutlery, Chianti bottle-lamp etc. (**Peggy**)

ACT II

SCENE 1

*On stage*:    As before

SCENE 2

*Set*:        Potted plant with no flowers

SCENE 3

*Strike*:          Potted plant with no flowers

SCENE 4

*On stage*:     As before

SCENE 5

*On stage*:     As before

SCENE 6

*On stage*:     As before

SCENE 7

*On stage*:     As before

SCENE 8

*On stage*:     As before

SCENE 9

*On stage*:     As before

SCENE 10

*On stage*:     As before

SCENE 11

*On stage*:     As before

SCENE 12

*On stage*:     As before

SCENE 13

*On stage*:     As before

SCENE 14

*On stage*:     As before

SCENE 15

*On stage*:    As before

SCENE 16

*Set*:        Mugs or glasses of red wine

*Off stage*:   Handful of postcards (**Steve**)

*Personal*:    **Heidi**: black eye patch
              **Steve**: sling

# LIGHTING PLOT

Property fittings required: nil

ACT I, SCENE 1

*To open*:        Spotlight on **Steve**

*No cues*

ACT I, SCENE 2

*To open*:        General interior lighting

*No cues*

ACT I, SCENE 3

*To open*:        Spotlight on **Irena**

*No cues*

ACT I, SCENE 4

*To open*:        General interior lighting

*No cues*

ACT I, SCENE 5

*To open*:        Spotlight on **Madge**

*No cues*

ACT I, SCENE 6

*To open*:        General interior lighting

*No cues*

ACT I, SCENE 7

*To open*:        Spotlight on **Jestin**

*No cues*

ACT I, SCENE 8

*To open*:        Spotlight on **Peggy**

*No cues*

ACT I, SCENE 9

*To open*:        Spotlight on **Steve**

*Cue* 1           The bell sounds                              (Page 14)
                  *Black-out*

ACT I, SCENE 10

*To open*:        Spotlight on **Jestin**

*Cue* 2           **Jestin** offers his hand to shake          (Page 15)
                  *Black-out*

ACT I, SCENE 11

*To open*:        General interior lighting

*No cues*

ACT I, SCENE 12

*To open*:        Dim interior night lighting; tower and cathedral dome lit
                  against a black sky

*Cue* 3           **Gennaro** turns on the overhead light      (Page 21)
                  *Bring up lights*

ACT I, SCENE 13

*To open*:        General interior lighting

*No cues*

ACT I, SCENE 14

| *To open*: | General interior lighting | |
|---|---|---|
| *Cue* 4 | **Madge**: "Queer bloody world, ain't it?" | (Page 27) |
| | *Black-out* | |

ACT I, SCENE 15

| *To open*: | Spotlight on **Irena** | |
|---|---|---|
| *Cue* 5 | **Irena**: "... you speak with a Russian accent." | (Page 28) |
| | *Black-out* | |

ACT I, SCENE 16

| *To open*: | Spotlight on **Madge** |
|---|---|
| *No cues* | |

ACT I, SCENE 17

| *To open*: | General interior lighting |
|---|---|
| *No cues* | |

ACT I, SCENE 18

| *To open*: | Spotlight on **Steve** | |
|---|---|---|
| *Cue* 6 | **Steve**: "We want the bakery." | (Page 32) |
| | *Black-out* | |

ACT I, SCENE 19

| *To open*: | Dim interior night lighting | |
|---|---|---|
| *Cue* 7 | **Steve** comes to **Heidi** from behind | (Page 36) |
| | *The lights change* | |
| *Cue* 8 | **Steve** turns out the lights | (Page 36) |
| | *Dim lights* | |

ACT II, SCENE 1

*To open*:      Spotlight on **Steve**

*Cue* 9          **Steve**: "Knocked 'em in the Old Kent Road."          (Page 37)
                 *Black-out*


ACT II, SCENE 2

*To open*:      Spotlight on **Madge**

*No cues*

ACT II, SCENE 3

*To open*:      General interior lighting

*No cues*

ACT II, SCENE 4

*To open*:      Spotlight on **Heidi**

*No cues*

ACT II, SCENE 5

*To open*:      Spotlight on **Steve**

*No cues*

ACT II, SCENE 6

*To open*:      General interior lighting

*No cues*

ACT II, SCENE 7

*To open*:      Spotlight on **Steve**

*No cues*

68                                          Lingua Franca

ACT II, Scene 8

*To open*:      General interior lighting

*No cues*

ACT II, Scene 9

*To open*:      Spotlight on **Madge**

*Cue* 10       **Madge**: "Not Yours Truly"                (Page 49)
               *Black-out*

ACT II, Scene 10

*To open*:      Spotlight on **Steve**

*Cue* 11       **Steve**: "Francesco — you try."          (Page 49)
               *Black-out*

ACT II, Scene 11

*To open*:      Spotlight on **Jestin**

*Cue* 12       **Jestin**: "Too advanced?"               (Page 50)
               *Fade spotlight almost to darkness*

ACT II, Scene 12

*To open*:      Dim interior night lighting. Through the window,
                lamplight on tower and cathedral dome

*Cue* 13       **Irena** turns the light on              (Page 50)
               *Bring lights up*

*Cue* 14       **Irena** turns the light off             (Page 50)
               *Dim lights*

ACT II, Scene 13

*To open*:      Spotlight on **Jestin**

*No cues*

ACT II, SCENE 14

*To open*:          General interior lighting

*Cue* 15          **Gennaro** hammers on the door                    (Page 53)
                  *Dazzling light directed at the audience*

*Cue* 16          **Gennaro** goes                                   (Page 54)
                  *Take out dazzling light*

ACT II, SCENE 15

*To open*:          Downstage lights are on

*No cues*

ACT II, SCENE 16

*To open*:          Evening interior lighting

*Cue* 17          **Irena**: "Sorridi!"                               (Page 55)
                  *Flash-bulb on* **Irena**, **Steve**, **Heidi**, **Madge** *and* **Gennaro**

# EFFECTS PLOT

Voices of students heard but not seen and voices heard from outside may be performed by actors off stage.

## ACT I

| | | |
|---|---|---|
| *Cue* 1 | To open SCENE 2<br>*Music of a street organ swells* | (Page 3) |
| *Cue* 2 | **Gennaro** shuts the window<br>*Music reduces from forte to piano* | (Page 3) |
| *Cue* 3 | **Gennaro** opens the window<br>*Volume of music increases* | (Page 5) |
| *Cue* 4 | **Peggy**: "... to hear there's no such animal."<br>*Music of street organ fades* | (Page 7) |
| *Cue* 5 | **Irena**: "... believed in once myself."<br>*Handbell rings* | (Page 8) |
| *Cue* 6 | **Irena**: "Yes, very nice."<br>*Bell rings* | (Page 9) |
| *Cue* 7 | **Madge**: "Leonardo — was ist das?"<br>*Bell rings* | (Page 10) |
| *Cue* 8 | To open SCENE 6<br>*The snarling of Vespas and blaring loudspeaker<br>announcements can be heard from the window* | (Page 10) |
| *Cue* 9 | **Steve** shuts the window<br>*Noise from the window decreases; sounds of many<br>Italian voices as students change classes* | (Page 10) |
| *Cue* 10 | **Steve**: "Steven Flowers."<br>*Bell rings* | (Page 11) |
| *Cue* 11 | **Steve**: "Fair enough. OK ..."<br>*Bell rings* | (Page 14) |

| | | |
|---|---|---|
| *Cue* 12 | Black-out<br>*The sound of student chatter as the classes change* | (Page 15) |
| *Cue* 13 | To open SCENE 12<br>*Street sounds can be heard* | (Page 18) |
| *Cue* 14 | **Heidi** shuts the window<br>*Sounds from the street reduce* | (Page 19) |
| *Cue* 15 | **Gennaro** opens the window<br>*Street sounds can be heard: scooters, voices, laughter* | (Page 21) |
| *Cue* 16 | **Heidi**: "... not having one of their own."<br>*Bell rings* | (Page 24) |
| *Cue* 17 | **Heidi**: "Heidi Schumann."<br>*Bell rings* | (Page 25) |
| *Cue* 18 | **Irena**: "I was so careful with the lamp."<br>*Bell rings* | (Page 28) |
| *Cue* 19 | **Madge** stares at the student for some moments<br>*Bell rings* | (Page 28) |
| *Cue* 20 | **Heidi** leaves by the washroom door<br>*Bell rings* | (Page 30) |
| *Cue* 21 | **Irena** goes. **Heidi** returns from the washroom<br>*There is a sound from the street* | (Page 31) |
| *Cue* 22 | To open SCENE 19<br>*Street sounds can be heard from the window* | (Page 32) |
| *Cue* 23 | The Lights change<br>*Bach chorale begins* | (Page 36) |

## ACT II

| | | |
|---|---|---|
| *Cue* 24 | **Peggy**: "Quite wasted as a teacher."<br>*Bell rings* | (Page 38) |
| *Cue* 25 | **Peggy**: "... Magdalenes everywhere else."<br>*Street organ and traffic sounds can be heard from<br>the window* | (Page 43) |
| *Cue* 26 | **Steve**: "Congratulazioni!"<br>*Bell rings* | (Page 44) |

*Cue* 27      **Steve**: "Leave it, Peg."                    (Page 47)
              *Bell rings*

*Cue* 28      To open SCENE 14                               (Page 51)
              *Music of the street organ*

*Cue* 29      **Gennaro** hammers on the door                (Page 53)
              *A climactic burst of Verdi*

*Cue* 30      To open SCENE 16                               (Page 55)
              *Street organ can be heard from the window*

*Cue* 31      Back projection of pictures of London          (Page 57)
              *Beatles music plays*

*Cue* 32      **Steve** goes on browsing through the cards   (Page 58)
              *Street organ plays "Yankee Doodle"*

USE OF COPYRIGHT MUSIC:

# Alan M. Kent

# OOGLY ES SIN

## The Lamentable Ballad of Anthony Payne Cornish Giant